World Tales for Family Storytelling III

51 Traditional Stories for Children
aged 8–11 years

Published by Hawthorn Press, Hawthorn House,
1 Lansdown Lane, Stroud, Gloucestershire, GL5 1BJ, UK
Tel: (01453) 757040 E-mail: info@hawthornpress.com
Website: www.hawthornpress.com

Illustrations © Shirin Adl
Cover design by Lucy Guenot
Typesetting by Winslade Graphics
Printed by Henry Ling Ltd, The Dorset Press

Printed on environmentally friendly chlorine-free paper sourced from renewable forest stock.

Every effort has been made to trace the ownership of all copyrighted material. If any omission has been made, please bring this to the publisher's attention so that proper acknowledgement may be given in future editions.

The views expressed in this book are not necessarily those of the publisher.

British Library Cataloguing in Publication Data applied for

ISBN 978-1-912480-67-8

Storytelling Series

World Tales for Family Storytelling III

51 Traditional Stories
for Children
aged 8–11 years

Chris Smith

Foreword by Sue Hollingsworth

Contents

Stories

Foreword

At a children's birthday party where I was telling stories, I remember a little girl of about six years old being so entranced by the story that she came closer and closer to me, eyes shining, until she was right by my side. When I'd finished, I turned to her and said, "Would you like to tell it now?" Immediately, she launched into her own version and all the other kids (including me!) listened to it again. She did a remarkable job, simplifying words, adding more to the scenes she loved and skimming over her least favourite bits. She was great!

From babies seeking eye contact and enjoying making babbling noises, to pre-schoolers trying to understand how jokes work: from organising games in the playground, to reading a story they've written, children want to connect, to communicate. But as they get older, it's often technology that they turn to and, with the power of social media, they can often feel isolated and unsupported. Many of them as adults never regain that pleasure in communication and connection for its own sake. As a teacher of storytelling to adults, I meet people who are afraid to stand up and tell a story, nervous about being looked at and really looking others in the eye. The vivid imagination of their childhoods and the pleasure and playfulness of the sound of their own voices has deserted them. They know something is missing and they long to find that magic again. This is our invisible cultural heritage, passed down generations by ordinary people like you and I for free. It is outside the market economy and yet hidden in its picture language are the secrets of how to live together with other humans and with the living world. Not moralistically pressed into lectures or lessons but painted into stories imbued with wonder.

So how can we as parents, grandparents and primary carers support our children to become confident adults, able to look a confusing and complex world in the eye? How can we help them make sense of overwhelming emotions, different ways of living and viewpoints and still stay connected? What can help instill in them a sense of worth and the joy of being alive in these troublesome times?

I believe you hold some of the answers to these questions in your hand right now. Stories have been humanity's biggest teachers since we first developed speech and long before writing was invented. All the traditional stories in this collection have stood the test of time, surviving in an oral form for many hundreds, if not thousands, of years before they were written down, because they had something to say to us about what it means to be fully human in this world. This wisdom has been passed on in story form because we all love stories, whatever age we are. As soon as we hear the magical words "Long, long ago" or "Once upon a time", we drop down into a deeply engaged space, hearts and ears open. Teachers are often amazed by how still and attentive even the most boisterous children become in the presence of a story well told. Parents or grandparents know the magic of telling or reading a child a story at bedtime. I can vividly remember the pleasure of having the undivided attention of my mother, the sound of her voice creating a sense of safety and security as I slipped into sleep. Nowadays I enjoy being with my grandchildren in the evenings, creating stories together, sharing their favourite books. Even as adults we are irresistibly drawn to stories in films, novels and music: we exchange the stories of our lives every day with our families, colleagues and friends.

But this book dares to go much, much further than merely offering a wonderful selection of stories for children. Not only are these stories suitable for reading out loud to children; not only are they wonderful for children to read themselves: these stories are especially crafted to encourage children to retell them, in their own way, just like the little girl at the birthday party did. And that's the secret ingredient! Once their attention shifts from looking at the page and reading the story, to looking at the listeners and retelling the story in their own words, that's when the magic begins to happen. In the retelling, the story becomes something that belongs to them, comes from within them, not just something they've read. In this way, the wisdom of the story is integrated in whatever way the child is ready for. But even more importantly, the child has to really focus on the listeners, to look into their eyes, to begin to gauge their reactions. They develop a sense of how to hold someone's attention, to read their body language and emotions. They experience the deep satisfaction of seeing someone they love laugh at their story, be moved by their story, want to hear more. They have a sense of themselves as someone who can speak and be listened to, of someone who has something worthwhile to say and ultimately, that they themselves are worthwhile. The confidence and sense of identity that this develops helps them face the challenges of peer group pressure, bullying, and rejection as they grow older. And all this happens whilst they are encouraged to be playful, imaginative and spontaneous – what a gift, and one that lasts their whole lives.

In an age when technology can seem to dominate our sense of what communication and connection looks like, let's hear it for the sound of children's voices telling stories. Let's support our children to look the world in the eye and speak out with confidence. Our future depends on it.

Sue Hollingsworth MBA

Storyteller, Coach & Consultant
www.suehollingsworth.com

Introduction

Storytelling in the home is a tried and tested way of helping your family to thrive. Since the dawn of language, humans have shared stories together in their families and tribes as a way of sharing information, learning language and bonding as a group. Our minds are hardwired to enjoy such story sharing. Some would say that our survival has depended on it.

What is meant by storytelling? In this volume the stories are intended to be told by an adult to a child or children, told jointly with the children joining in in various ways, or told independently by the child to an adult or to other children in the family. The main idea is to retell them from memory in the storyteller's own words, rather than read them out word-for-word although the stories can also be read if you wish.

Such storytelling will have a host of benefits for your children and your family, helping your children master new language, ideas and emotions while building their confidence in communication. Storytelling can also create a safe, intimate, special time for being together.

Seven important benefits of home storytelling are:

- Language – a way of actively building vocabulary, comprehension and communication skills, not just by listening but by actively using language;

- Ideas – a way of engaging with ideas about the wider world beyond our own direct experience;

- Emotions – a way to explore empathy and emotion through putting ourselves in a character's shoes;

- Creativity – a way of building up the creative imagination of a child through the images and ideas of the stories themselves;

- Confidence – a way to help children become confident communicators through storytelling as they learn that their voice is valued by others and can be a pleasure to hear;

- Intimacy – a way to create a supportive and loving space for story sharing and story play;
- Values – a way to introduce and explore values through story.

Inside this volume you will find a set of 'World Stories' for reading, retelling and reflecting upon in the family. They are all 'traditional' meaning they have come from the spoken word tradition of storytelling. All will have been shared as spoken word and retold in various ways in families and communities around the globe. Such stories evolve with time as new tellers add their own ideas and twists to the tale, and are suited to spoken word telling: easy to remember and easy to retell.

They are here to share within your family in whatever way you choose: read them, tell them from memory, change them, re-enact them, discuss them, paint them, play with them and above all get your family to engage with them. You can find ideas for ways to do this in *Smith and Barron (2020) 147 Storytelling Games and Creative Activities for the Classroom and the Home.*

One simple way to teach your child to tell these stories is by using the Hear-Map-Step-Speak (HMSS):
- First read or tell the story to your children.
- Then have each draw a little map of the main events.
- After that practice 'stepping' through the story with a gesture and phrase for each step.
- Finally have a go at telling the story, using the map and gestures to aid memory.

For more details about HMSS and other aspects of the Storytelling Schools method see *Smith, Guillain and Barron (2020) The Storytelling Schools Method: Handbook for Teachers.*

This book is popular with parents who use storytelling at home. You might also have a look at the HMSS section on the Storytelling Schools YouTube channel.

These stories come from a collection of traditional stories for use in primary schools called *147 Traditional Stories for Primary School Children to Retell* (Smith, second edition 2021). The main idea was to provide a set of tried and tested stories as a springboard for learning. Since then, the stories have travelled to schools around the globe, providing a tried and tested way of learning language, communication and creativity. In 2020/21 during COVID lockdown, for example, more than four million online lessons were downloaded which used these stories as the starting point.

I hope that you and your family enjoy exploring these stories together. You will then join the countless storytellers around the globe who have told and retold these tales over the centuries. May they continue to bring pleasure, learning and community to families around the globe.

Although the book is notionally for children aged 8–11 years, all of these tales can be adapted for a wide range of ages. Also, the content of traditional stories reflects the time and place in which the stories evolved. Some tales may include behaviour or ideas which are at odds with modern values, for example concerning attitudes to gender, marriage and human rights in general. Where this occurs the stories provide an opportunity for you as a parent to discuss and reflect on this with your child.

1. The Hunter and the Leopard

This is a brilliant African story about cruelty and payback. There's a great text version in McCall Smith's The Girl Who Married a Lion. *I once heard Jan Blake tell this story – it was unforgettable. Here we conjure the environment of the African jungle, the hubris of the hunter and the fierce predator power of the leopard woman.*

Once there was a hunter. He was a proud hunter. He loved to kill the fiercest wild animals – lions, tigers and pumas. The thrill of the danger was like a drug for him. He'd carry the bodies of his kill through the village and show them to everyone.

'Am I not the best hunter?' he'd ask with a smile.
'Oh yes, you are the best!' they'd reply.

One springtime the hunter took time off from his hunting to find himself a wife. Soon he was married and soon his wife's belly began to swell with child. After nine moons a healthy baby boy was born. The hunter was delighted.

'We will celebrate!' he shouted to his visitors. 'At the naming ceremony I will bring a leopard cub and sacrifice it to the gods.'

The people were impressed – to steal a live leopard cub was dangerous, very dangerous. If the mother leopard caught you she would kill you for sure.

'Are you sure?' they said.
'Oh yes,' he said. 'I will do it!'

He trekked off to the deepest, darkest part of the forest and searched for leopard tracks. After a week he found the tracks of a mother and two cubs and followed them, silent as night, till he reached their cave. Hiding downwind he waited for the mother to go out hunting then ran into the cave, scooped up the sleeping cubs, popped them in his sack and ran back to the village where he put them in a cage in his hut.

'Tomorrow,' he said to himself, 'they will die. The naming ceremony of my boy will be remembered for ever.'

Deep in the forest the mother leopard returned to an empty cave. She smelt the smell of the hunter.

'Man!' she growled. 'Are my children still alive?'

She found the hunter's tracks and followed them to the door of his hut. There she stood up on hind legs and peeled off her leopard skin. Inside, was the body of a beautiful young woman with a leopard skin wrapped around her hips. Her hair was long and dark and her eyes black and fierce. Hiding the peeled skin behind a tree, she knocked on the hunter's door.

The hunter opened the door and smiled at her.
'Hello,' he said. 'Who are you?'
'I am lost,' she said, smiling at the hunter. 'I have nowhere to stay tonight. I am frightened, can you help me?'
'Oh yes,' said the hunter, 'you can spend the night in my hut if you like!'
'Oh thank you,' she said, fluttering her long dark lashes. 'How can I ever thank you?'
'Oh, I'll think of something!' he said, grinning. 'Come on in!'

They sat together in the hut and drank some palm wine. In the next room the cubs were whining.

'What's that noise?' she asked.

'I caught two leopard cubs,' he said proudly. 'Tomorrow, at my son's naming ceremony, I will sacrifice them. It will be remembered for ever.'

Suddenly she began to cry. 'Please don't!' she said. 'Please spare their lives! I'll do anything for you if you let them live!'

The hunter was angry.

'Get out of my hut!' he shouted. 'And don't come back till you stop crying. I have promised to kill the cubs and I will kill them!'

She stepped outside for a moment, slipped into her leopard skin and leaped back onto the hunter as a leopard, ripping out his throat before he could reach for his knife. She went to her children, smashed the cage with a blow of her paw and led them back to the cave.

The next morning the whole village waited for the hunter to come, but he could not. They found his body ripped and torn on the floor of the hut.

So it was that the ceremony was remembered in the village for many years. Indeed it is even told by storytellers to this very day!

2. The Boots of Abu Kassim

This story is hugely popular in the Middle East as a much-loved parable about generosity. Mean old Abu Kassim sees his fortune disappear as his meanness bears fruit. The plot is fairly absurd and can be played for comedy. Let Abu Kassim get more and more animated as his doom deepens.

Once there was a rich man called Abu Kassim. He was a rich merchant but was mean and just saved and never spent. His old boots were full of holes and covered in patches, but he was too mean to buy himself some new ones. They were famous boots. If something needed replacing people would say, 'Now that's just like Abu Kassim's boots!' and everyone would understand.

Abu Kassim was so mean that he only took a bath once a year at the public baths in the centre of town. More than once was too expensive, he thought. One time he was taking his annual bath when, for a joke, someone swapped his old boots for the fine shoes of the Chief Judge, which were left in the next cubicle.

When Abu Kassim had finished his bath he went back to change and saw the fine new shoes. He smiled, thinking the new shoes were a gift, and wore them home happily, thinking that by waiting to change his old boots he had saved quite a few pennies.

But when the Judge had finished bathing he saw the old boots with his clothes and knew immediately who the owner was. Abu Kassim was summoned to the court wearing the Judge's shoes.

'You stole my boots!' the Judge thundered. 'So you must pay a fine of 100 dinars, or spend a month in prison.'

It was very painful for Abu Kassim to pay the fine but he couldn't afford to go to jail. He paid the 100 dinars and walked home with his old boots, fuming.

Walking by the river he cursed the boots and threw them in the river.

'I never want to see you again!' he said.

Some fishermen were fishing downstream, and the old boots caught in their nets. The nails in the boots cut the nets to shreds. When the fishermen saw the boots they recognised them immediately.

'Abu Kassim!' they shouted. They went round to his house and threw the boots in through his window.

Abu Kassim had just bought a crate of glass bottles and a case of expensive perfume and had just finished filling the bottles. He was set to make 1,000 dinars from the sale of the perfume in the fancy bottles. Just then his boots flew in through the window and smashed all the bottles to pieces.

'Oh no!' he shouted at the boots. 'How could you do that to me? You have cost me 1,000 dinars!'

He put his wet boots up on the roof to dry but a dog on the roof started playing with the boots and knocked them down onto the head of a woman walking in the street below. She was pregnant and the boots hit her so hard that she lost the baby.

Abu Kassim was summoned to the court and ordered to pay 10,000 dinars to the family of the woman in compensation. That was all of his wealth.

He sold his house and business and paid the fine, cursing his boots as he did it.

Then he went to the Judge and handed over the boots, saying that from this day, whatever the boots did was not his responsibility.

Instead he opened a shoe shop in the market and would stand in the doorway, telling this story when people walked past wearing worn-out boots. In this way his business thrived. From then on he always wore a nice clean pair of shoes.

3. Who is the Thief?

This Japanese story is a great way of introducing crime-solving plots, and shows how this can be done in an unexpected and interesting way. You can find a lovely text version of this by Susan Klein in Holt's Ready-To-Tell Tales. Pay attention to the wording of the Judge's lines as you tell this. You have to get it fairly precise for the desired effect. Linger with the moment when the stone is accused and the people protest. Let the audience be puzzled for a while.

Once there was a city. In that city was a bakery, and in the bakery – a baker. Every day he'd get up in the middle of the night, mix up the flour, salt, yeast and sugar, knead it into smooth dough and wait for it to rise. When the dough was ready he'd cut it into small pieces and fry them in hot oil to make oilbread. At dawn he'd put the oily breads in a basket and carry it to the market where he would always sell out – they were delicious and a real treat!

One morning he had sold all the bread, and had a pile of crisp yen notes in his basket. He walked up the hill behind the market, sat next to a large stone and counted his money before putting it back in the basket. Then, a little weary, he closed his eyes and fell asleep.

When he woke up the money was gone. Furious, he ran back down to the market calling out, 'There's a thief! There's a thief in the market! Someone has stolen my money! Beware!'

The shopkeepers crowded around him clutching their money pouches tight to their bellies.

'I sold my breads, put the money in my breadbasket and went to sleep by the stone up the hill. When I woke up the money was gone!'

The shopkeepers were frightened now – what if it happened to them? They started arguing and shouting about what to do and even eyed each other suspiciously, wondering if one of the shopkeepers was the thief.

'Let's ask the Judge,' said the baker. 'He'll know what to do.'
The baker went off to the Judge's house and was soon sitting in his front room drinking tea.

'Please listen to my story and see if you can help. I was in the marketplace today selling fried dough. I sold everything and climbed the hill for a rest. I put my basket on the stone there, counted the money, put it back in the basket and fell asleep, and when I woke up the money had gone. There's a thief in the market!'

The Judge stroked his chin. 'Tell me again,' he said. The baker repeated his story.

'Again.'

'So!' said the Judge. 'You sold your dough, climbed the hill, counted the money, put it in the basket on the stone and fell asleep, and when you woke up the money was gone.'

'Yes!' said the baker, feeling a little impatient.

'Let's go to the place where you slept.'

The baker and Judge walked through the market and up the hill to the stone, followed by a crowd of excited shopkeepers. When they were all there, the shopkeepers were chattering excitedly.

'Quiet!' thundered the Judge. 'This is the situation. The baker sold his dough, he climbed the hill, counted the money, went to sleep and when he woke up the money was gone. There is a thief in the market!'

Everyone started talking excitedly at once.

'SILENCE!' shouted the Judge. 'I have thought it all through and the answer is simple. If the baker put the money in the basket and the basket on the stone and then fell asleep, then the stone must have taken the money. The stone did it! That is the solution. Let us arrest the stone.'

All the shopkeepers were shouting at once, unable to believe that the Judge would talk such rubbish.

'QUIET!' he bellowed. 'How dare you disrespect me? I am the Judge. How dare you! You must all be punished!'

The shopkeepers fell to their knees and apologised, all at the same time.

'QUIET!' he shouted. 'Each of you will spend three days in jail for your impertinence!'

'Please, NO!' they all wailed. 'We need to feed our families! Have mercy!'

'Very well,' said the Judge. 'I will show mercy, but each of you must pay a twenty yen fine for your rudeness.'

He shouted at the baker. 'Go and get me a bucketful of hot water. Now!'

The baker brought back a steaming bucket and placed it in front of the Judge.

'Now, each of you put twenty yen into the bucket.'

One by one, as the Judge watched, each shopkeeper threw a twenty yen note into the bucket and then went on his way. One by one until... a young man tossed a note into the bucket. Immediately the Judge roared out, 'YOU! You are the thief! Arrest him!'

The Judge was right, but how did he know? (Hint: oil floats on water)

4. Beowulf

Beowulf is one of the classics of early English literature. The original text is a huge epic poem about killing first the monster and then its mother. It is a hero story about monster-killing, so you have to get into that kind of world.
Below are the bare bones: expand it any way you like.

Once, a great Danish king built a great hall so that all of his vast army could eat and drink under one roof. His men were singing and drinking long into the night, which disturbed a ferocious monster that lived nearby – Grendel.

The monster waited until the men were sleeping and then, creeping into the hall, he killed thirty men where they lay. After that the Danes lived in fear of this monster that would come from time to time and take a few lives. No one could think of a way to defeat the monster.

Then Prince Beowulf, strongest of warriors, decided he would fight the monster. He set sail with twelve men and arriving at the Danish king's hall he was warmly welcomed. That evening they held a feast in his honour. Beowulf promised he would kill the monster or be killed trying.

Later that night, when the men were falling asleep, Grendel appeared ready to kill a few men, but Beowulf, not even bothering with a sword, leapt on the monster and started to wrestle him. The fight went on for hours until Beowulf got a firm grip and ripped off the monster's arm and claw. Grendel ran away back to his lake, leaving his bloody arm in Beowulf's hand.

The Danes were delighted with their new hero and sang his praises long into the night, feasting again till morning.

The next night, when all were sleeping, a stronger monster, the mother of Grendel, came to the hall and took away one of the Danes together with her son's claw.

When Beowulf woke up he followed the monster's tracks to the lake. Above the lake on a rock was the bloody head of the kidnapped Dane.

This time, taking a sword, Beowulf dived down to the mother's home under the lake. There was a long and terrible battle. Both were fearsome and fought to the death. In the end Beowulf killed her with his sword and then chopped off the head of her son for good measure.

After this battle Beowulf returned to the Danish court and told his story, and after another feast and gifts of great treasures Beowulf returned home with his men, leaving Denmark free from the fear of Grendel and his terrible mother.

And that's how Beowulf saved the Danes from not one, but two monsters.

5. The Tiger's Whisker

This gentle and surprising story about patience and understanding comes from Indonesia, and is often told as a parable for parents giving their kids a bit of space. There's a fine telling in Courlander's book of the same name. You need to evoke the pain of the mother, then her skill and patience with the tiger. Pause when the whisker goes in the fire and keep the tension there before delivering the punchline. It's a chance to evoke the mountains and tigers of Indonesia.

Once there was a mother and a daughter. They loved each other and delighted in each other's company, telling each other stories and secrets like two sisters. But, one day when the daughter reached that age when she was no longer a little girl, she stopped speaking to her mother. It happened after an argument about something or other, and the girl just stopped speaking.

'Talk to me!' said the mother. 'Let me help you! Tell me what the matter is. I am your mother.'

But the girl said nothing.

The mother grew angry. 'Don't be so rude. Talk! Say something!' But the girl said nothing.

The mother started to cry. 'How can you treat me like this after all I have done for you?' The girl left the room.

Desperate, the mother went off to the wise woman of the forest to ask her advice. Inside her hut, the old lady was sitting on a three-legged stool smoking a long black pipe.

'My daughter won't talk to me! What shall I do?'

The old lady stared long and hard at the tearful mother. 'Bring me a whisker from the angry tiger who lives at the top of the mountain.'

So the mother went home, had a think, made a plan, packed a sack full of meat and climbed up the mountain. She dropped a piece of meat about a hundred paces from the entrance to the tiger's cave, hid behind a rock, and waited. A while later the tiger came out, huge and fierce, sniffing the air nervously. He padded over to the meat, picked it up in his razor teeth, and padded back into the cave.

The mother waited all day and all night behind the rock, then the next morning she put out another piece of meat, this time fifty paces from the cave. Again the tiger padded out, picked up the meat and went back into the cave.

She waited another day and put the meat twenty-five paces from the cave. The next day ten paces.

This time when the tiger came out she showed herself standing and watching in the distance as the tiger took the meat. The tiger eyed her curiously.

The next day she was a little closer and the next closer still until after two weeks she stood outside the cave with the meat at her feet.

As the tiger bent down to pick up his food she stroked his neck and purred to him. He waited for a while before returning to the cave.

The next day she held the meat. The tiger came and ate from her hand as she sang to him. As he ate she reached out slowly and pulled out one of his white whiskers. He was so busy eating the meat he hardly noticed.

That afternoon she returned to the hut of the wise woman brandishing her whisker.

'Here's the whisker,' she said triumphant. 'Take it!'

The wise woman took the whisker and threw it onto the fire.

'Why did you do that?' asked the mother.

'Now you are ready. It took great skill and patience to get that whisker,' replied the wise woman. 'Now use those same skills at home.'

The mother went home and for a week she said nothing to her daughter, keeping busy with other things, just sharing a silent meal every evening. Then she started to sing to her at bedtime asking for nothing in return. Slowly the daughter softened and relaxed and with time, in her time, they began to talk again.

6. The Apple Tree Man

This story is popular among English storytellers, especially in autumn for the apple harvest and in winter during the New Year period. You can find it told in various traditional folk songs, too. The climax of the story is the final scene when the animals make a fool of the greedy brother. Get the animals and mean brother well into character to make that moment work.

Once there was a farm where a farmer lived with his two sons. The eldest, Jack, was a quiet boy who didn't talk much, but worked hard and well. The youngest, John, was always talking and joking and worked when he wished and not when he didn't. The father loved the youngest most, enjoying his charm and style, and somehow found the elder son a disappointment. The farmer was prudent and careful and saved a great deal of money, which he kept hidden in a secret place. He told no one about it.

In the evenings, when the boys were young, he'd tell them stories around the fire. Their favourite was a tale about talking animals in which all the farm animals talked to each other about this and that.

Sometimes he'd say to his boys, 'If you want to know where my treasure is hidden, listen to the donkey and cow talking at midnight on Christmas Eve. That's the one time when you can hear them talk. They know everything about the farm. Maybe they'll tell you where the treasure is.'

When the farmer died he left the farm and land to John, the younger son. John promptly hired a manager to run the business and lived a life of ease. Jack inherited nothing, and John rented him a small piece of land for the rent of one silver shilling a year. Jack's piece of land was just ten paces square, with a tumbledown cottage, an apple tree, an old cow and an even older donkey. Jack lived there, tending to the tree, making cider from its apples, milking the cow, making cheese from its milk, and growing vegetables to make ends meet as best he could. He cared for the cow and donkey with love, finding them the best food and straw and rubbing oils and herbs into their hides to make them well.

Every year in midwinter, when the cider was almost finished, Jack would pour the cider dregs onto the tree's roots and sing it a song:

> *Apple tree, apple tree,*
> *I give to you just as you give to me.*
> *Apple tree, apple tree,*
> *Blessings on your harvest!*

Every Christmas Day Jack would pay his silver shilling to his brother, who had grown fat and greedy with the passing years.

One Christmas Eve John came to visit his brother's cottage. 'You owe me a shilling for rent,' he said, impatiently.

Jack shook his head. 'Sorry, I don't have any money. Can you wait till I sell the next set of cheeses in a couple of weeks?'

'No!' snapped John. 'Pay up tomorrow or you're out!'

Just then, John remembered his father's story about the donkey and cow talking.

'Wait a minute,' he said. 'I'll tell you what, Jack, you wake me up at midnight and I'll come and listen to your animals. Maybe they'll tell me where my treasure is buried.'

That evening Jack fed the animals, bedded them down in the hut and took the last of the year's cider and poured it over the roots of the apple tree singing to the tree:

Apple tree, apple tree...

Just then the trunk of the tree seemed to shimmer and shift in front of his eyes. One moment there was a tree trunk, the next a man stepped out of the trunk. He was as worn and wrinkled and knobbly as the old apple tree, with skin like tree bark, rosy red cheeks and long green hair. Jack wanted to run, but the apple tree man said, 'Wait, my friend! All these years you have looked after me as if I was your child with love and care. Now it's my turn to look after you. Your father's treasure is buried under my roots. Dig it up and you will be rich. But keep it quiet – your brother is greedy and jealous and he would try and steal it.'

Jack took a shovel and sure enough, down under the roots where he had poured the cider, there was a chest filled with gold and silver. Jack took it and hid it in his cottage and waited.

At midnight he went to his brother's mansion and woke him up. 'It's midnight, brother!'

'Good. Now go away! I want to listen to these animals by myself!'

John went over to the animal hut and peeped in at the window. The two animals were awake. One moment they were mooing and braying, the next he could hear the meanings of their sounds. They were speaking! The story was true!

The cow said, 'Hey, Donkey. Happy Christmas!'
'Thanks, Cow. Happy Christmas to you!'
'What's new with you?'
'Nothing, what's new with you?'

They chatted about straw and grass and the weather for ages while John listened impatiently.

'What about the treasure? What about the treasure?' he thought.

Finally the donkey laughed. 'You know the old man's treasure?'
'Yup!' laughed the cow.
'You know where it is?' asked the donkey.
'Yup!' laughed the cow.
'Are you going to tell me?'

John was excited now. Finally he'd get his hands on the treasure.

'Nope!' said the cow, chuckling.
'Why's that then?'
'Because that selfish so and so, John, is listening at the window and he doesn't deserve it. All his life he's just helped himself and never anyone else. So I think I'll just keep quiet!'
'Good plan!' laughed the donkey.

John jumped up and shouted out, 'Tell me!' but after that all he could hear were moos and brays.

Christmas Day came and Jack went round to visit his brother. 'Happy Christmas, John,' he said smiling. 'Here's your shilling!'

'Where did you get that?' John asked suspiciously, but Jack just smiled.

Within the year Jack had bought his brother's farm from him, and he looked after the land with care and love. And every Christmas Eve he'd go to that old apple tree, pour some cider on the roots and sing to the tree:

> *Apple tree, apple tree...*

7. Godmother Death

This is a story about trying to trick Death, and learning to accept it. It comes from Mexico and is associated there with the Mexican Day of the Dead. It speaks of issues of poverty and injustice and has a powerful twist at the end. Develop the characters of Death and the son.

Riddle: What has one head, one foot, and four legs?
Answer: A bed.

Once, on the edge of a capital city, there was a sprawling shanty of huts and tents where the poorest of the city lived. In one of those huts there lived a husband and his pregnant wife. As her belly grew and grew the worries of the father grew with it.

'How can I look after this child and offer him a good life? How can I give him power, when the poor are powerless? How can I give him justice when all the poor know is injustice? The poor children starve while the rich play with golden toys. How can I give him mercy? For the poor the world is brutal and unmerciful.'

The man's son was born on the Day of the Dead, the luckiest day of the year to be born in Mexico. That same day, the father went off to look for a godmother for him, walking around the streets of the shanty town. 'I want someone,' he thought, 'who can give him those three things: mercy, justice and power.' He put his wish in a song:

Who will be godmother for my son?
Who will do that for me?
Who can give him what he needs,
Power, justice and mercy?

He walked and walked, singing his song. A rich carriage rolled by pulled by four fine horses. It stopped by the father and a rich lady looked out with gold around her neck and furs on her shoulders. 'That's a lovely song,' she said. 'Why do you sing it?'

'I'm looking for a godmother for my son. He was born today, the Day of the Dead!'

'Oh! Well, I could be his godmother. I can give him riches and power.'

'No thanks,' said the father. 'You rich people have power, but know little of justice or mercy. You eat while we starve. That is not suitable for a boy born on the Day of the Dead.'

The father continued on his way, singing the song: **Who will be godmother...**

He walked past a woman dressed in rags. 'That's a lovely song,' she said. 'Why do you sing it?'

'I'm looking for a godmother for my son, born today, the Day of the Dead!'

'Oh! Well, I could be his godmother. I can teach him mercy and justice.'

'No thanks,' said the father. 'You are poor so you know much about justice and mercy, but you are powerless. We starve and there is little you can do. That is not suitable for a boy born on the Day of the Dead.'

The father continued on his way, singing the song: **Who will be godmother...**

He came across a tall thin woman wrapped up in a dark cloak. He could not see her face.

'Let me be the godmother,' she said in a dark, even voice.

'Who are you?' said the man, with a chill in his belly.

'I am Death!'

He brightened up immediately. 'Death! Mmm... Death has mercy – when suffering is too much you bring relief. Death shows justice – coming to all whether rich or poor. And Death has power – no one is stronger than Death. Yes, you can be my son's godmother.'

The baby grew into a child and the child into a man. One day his godmother visited him and took him into the woods. 'You see this herb?' she said. 'It is called the herb of life. Take it and crush it and you will heal the sick. Use it unless you see me at the head of the bed.' The young man nodded.

With this gift the young man became a healer, using his power for good for the rich and poor alike. He became well known and well respected for his powers.

One day the king's daughter fell sick. No healer could help her. Her father was desperate and offered half his kingdom to anyone who could heal her, so the young man turned up at the palace with his herb. When he got to the princess's room he was disappointed – Death was standing at the head of the bed. What should he do?

Then he had an idea. 'Turn the bed around quickly!' he called. 'The princess must face the window!'

They twisted the bed around so that Death was at the foot of the bed and he slipped in a drop of herb before Death could move. Death glowered at the young man and disappeared.

The princess was soon healed and the young man became wealthy beyond dreams. He spent his time in the palace and soon won the love of the princess. They planned to marry but a week before the wedding she fell sick again. He went to her bed with his herb, and again saw Death at the head of the bed. Again he turned the bed around and healed her as Death looked on.

The day after the wedding Death came to visit the young man. 'Come with me!' she said. The young man followed Death out of town and down a tunnel into the deep earth. They entered a grave filled with flickering lights – some going out and some bursting into life.

'These are the lives of people,' said Death. 'When the light goes out, the life has ended… This is yours.' She pointed to a candle that had almost finished – just a liquid pool of wax was left on the rock.

'No! Godmother! Please show me mercy. I am just married!'

'I have shown you mercy. Twice you disobeyed me and I did not punish you. I have given you power, I have given you mercy. Now it is time for justice!'

Death bent down and blew out the candle.

8. The Weaver's Dream

I love the way this Chinese story plays with the idea of stories and imagination making dreams come true. It can link into all sorts of art projects, creating the images in the story. Make sure your children know all about weaving before you tell it. It switches into wonder in the final scene. Tell that with amazement.

Once there was a poor widow who lived with her three sons in a little shack on the edge of town. Every day she sat at her loom weaving – threading the shuttle back and forth between the threads. As she wove she sang:

> *I'm weaving the warp and weaving the thread.*
> *I'll weave and weave until I am dead.*
> *I weave and weave with fingers swift.*
> *My life is weaving – that's my gift.*

Every day she'd weave from dawn to dusk until her fingers were so tired she could work no more. In this way she made just enough money to feed her three sons. Two of her sons thought little of this. Their mother was just the way she was – they had never known any different. The youngest, however, saw how hard she worked and wished he could help.

One night the weaver-mother had a dream. In the dream there was a fine house, a wonderful garden, a glimmering lake and a golden shining sun above high white mountains. When she woke she was delighted by its beauty and resolved to weave it into her next cloth.

Every day she sat at her loom pushing and pulling the threads until, after a year and a day, the cloth was ready. It was the finest thing she had ever made and she was proud as she showed her sons. 'We'll keep it!' she said. 'This is my dream home. When I look at it I will be at peace.'

Just then a wind picked up the cloth and lifted it up out of the window and into the sky, high away onto the hills. The widow cried and cried as her sons clustered around. 'Bring me the cloth,' she said, 'or I will die!'

She took to her bed and refused to eat, just staring at the wall.

The eldest son set off on the path into the hills and after three days he came to an old lady sitting under a peach tree heavy with fruit. Next to her was an old stone horse.

'Where are you going?' the old lady asked.

'To find my mother's cloth,' he said.

'It's been taken by the mountain goddess,' the old lady said. 'But I'll tell you how to get it back – knock out your two front teeth and put them in the stone horse's mouth. Then he will come alive and fly you through the Land of Fire and then the Land of Ice. It's very hot and very cold, but if you live you'll get to the goddess's palace. Then you can ask her for the cloth back.'

The son said he didn't really want to knock out his teeth and asked if there was some other way to get his mother's cloth back.

'Fine!' the old lady said, 'Take this box of gold home and your mother will no longer be poor.'

The eldest walked down the hill with the box of gold, but, ashamed to admit his failure, and rather fond of the gold, he bought a house in a village elsewhere and never went home.

After a while the middle son went off to look for the cloth. He met the old lady and got the same speech.

'I'm not sure about the Lands of Fire and Ice,' he said. 'Isn't there another way?'

The old lady smiled and gave him a box of gold for his mother, and he set off for home. Full of shame and greed, he settled in the same village as his brother.

By this time the mother was as thin as a needle and never smiled at all. The youngest went off in search of the cloth and met the same old lady on the road. She gave the same speech and without hesitation he knocked out his teeth with a rock and stuck them into the stone horse's mouth. As it came alive the youngest son jumped on the horse's back and flew off to the east. They passed through fire and passed through ice, and then came to the palace of the mountain goddess.

The son walked into the palace and saw a beautiful woman standing next to a loom where a weaver was working. Next to the loom was his mother's cloth. He wasn't sure which was more beautiful, the cloth or the woman, but he said, 'Please may I take back the cloth? If not my mother will die.'

'Just a few more hours,' said the goddess. 'I love the picture so much. When we have finished copying it you may take it home.'

The son waited and watched until he fell asleep. While he slept the copy was finished but the goddess could not bear to lose the original. She told the weaver to put it back on the loom and weave her picture into it. The weaver did so and then the goddess rolled up the cloth, woke up the son and gave it back to him.

He flew back to the old lady, took the teeth out of the horse and walked home with the cloth. The mother was delighted. 'Thank you, son,' she said, smiling. 'Oh look! There's a lovely lady there now. I wonder who she is?'

At that moment the wind picked up the cloth and it flew out the window.

'Oh, no! Not again!' said the son.

Mother and son rushed outside, but this time the cloth hung in the air as if held by invisible hands.

As they watched the cloth began to grow – larger and larger until it stretched from the earth to the sky. One minute it was a cloth and then the next minute it was gone. In its place was a golden sun, white mountains, a beautiful garden and, behind them, a wonderful house. Sitting on a seat by the lake was the goddess.

The son was delighted and married the goddess on the spot. The three lived happily in their lovely dream home.

As for the brothers, they lived miserably until they died, never returning to their family home.

Too bad for them!

9. The Prince and the Birds

Here's a charming Spanish wondertale, with a chance to practise your poetry. It's set in the amazing Alhambra in Granada, so lots of background research is possible here. The prince travels around Spain so you can map out his journeys later. There are lots of twists and turns in this one. Enjoy.

If you were ever to travel from where you are right now, north, south, east and west, until you come to a country called Spain, and if you continued with your journey to a town called Granada and if you climbed the hill in the city you would come to the Palace of Al Hambra, one of the most wonderful buildings on the Earth. If you were to enter its gates and explore its gardens and pools and beautifully decorated chambers, you might enter the Jannat al Arif – also known as the Summer Palace.

You might wander through the water garden with its water channels and fountains, surrounded by blossoms and fruit and vines, or explore the empty rooms of the palace, a labyrinth of arches and wonderful decorated ceilings. Each view breathtaking. Each view a celebration of life and God.

If you were to meet the storyteller who still sells his stories in the palace, and were to ask him for a story, and if he understood that your heart was searching for happiness, you might just be lucky enough to hear this story...

Once, in the city of Granada, at the time of Muslim rule, there lived a king who liked to hold on tight to the things that he loved. He loved his palace, he loved his kingdom and he dealt firmly with anyone who challenged his rule. Heads rolled from those bodies which displeased him.

When his first son, Ahmed, was born, the Royal Astrologer read the patterns in the stars and in the entrails of three eagles and reported the results to the king. 'One day,' he predicted, 'your son will fall in love with a foreign girl from a distant land and leave the palace to win her hand.'

This thought took root in the king's mind. He imagined his son as a young man leaving him and never coming back. He imagined being without an heir to his throne. He imagined a lonely old age. Year by year these thoughts grew and grew until, on Ahmed's third birthday, he ordered that his son should live in the Summer Palace behind closed walls and that he should know nothing of the world of women.

So Ahmed grew up behind closed walls, in a palace of unsurpassed beauty. He spent his time wandering the gardens of the palace, bathing in its pools and gazing from its windows. All he knew was the world of men. They tilled his garden, brought him his food, and they taught him. An old whitebeard was his tutor-teacher and friend. Anyone who entered the palace was sworn to secrecy about the existence of women on pain of death.

When Ahmed reached the age when he was no longer a child, but not yet a man, he became restless. In his dreams he saw images from his early years, the sights and touch and scent of the women who had cared for him. He did not know what they were but he woke every morning with an ache in his belly and a longing for something other than the flowers and fountains and beautiful views. With this longing he became ill and thin and pale.

When news of his sadness reached the king the old tutor was summoned.

'What's the matter with my son?' asked the king,
as the whole court listened.

'He is unhappy,' answered the whitebeard,
carefully.

'Yes! But why?' snapped the king.

The old man thought for a minute and frowned. 'He wants to marry a dragon
and kill a beautiful princess.'

Everyone laughed at the old man's stupidity. Then the king scowled and everyone
held their breath.

'You are dismissed!' he shouted.

The old man thanked the king and left the palace with a grin on his face, leaving
the prince without his friend and mentor.

From that day Ahmed grew sadder and sadder. He spent his time wandering
the gardens and writing poems, which no one ever read. One day a white dove
perched on his window sill. Ahmed left corn on the sill for the bird to eat and
soon it was feeding out of his hands. Wanting to keep the bird as a friend he
popped it in a golden cage, but that evening he saw that there were tears in the
dove's eyes.

'What's the matter?' Prince Ahmed asked. 'Don't you like your cage?'

'I miss my Love,' said the bird.

'What's Love?' asked the prince.

'Misery for one and happiness for two,' answered the bird. 'Good when together
and sad when apart. Please let me go!'

The prince opened the cage and the dove flew away, leaving the prince deep in
thought.

'Maybe that's why I am sad,' he thought. 'Maybe I need Love too?'

A few days later the dove returned to the palace. 'Now I can help you,' it said. 'In a castle to the north there is a sad and lonely princess, as fair as a field of ripe wheat, with eyes as bright as cornflowers. Why don't you write her a letter?' The Prince sat and, putting pen to paper, he wrote her a poem. The dove took it and flew off.

A while later the dove returned at dusk, but as it approached the window a huntsman's arrow flew up from the field below and pierced its heart. It fell onto the sill, a bundle of white feathers and red blood, and died in the prince's hands. Around its neck the prince saw a necklace and locket. When he opened the locket there was the face of a woman as fair as a field of golden wheat, with eyes like cornflowers.

That evening he slipped out of the window, down the drainpipe and out into the garden to the old hollow oak where the wise old owl lived. Prince Ahmed showed the owl the locket and asked for help.
'I will take you to my aunt in Seville,' said the owl. 'She is the wisest old bird I know.'

Together they left the garden and climbed the mountains until after weeks of journeying they reached Seville. The owl aunt was perched in the attic of a fine palace when they arrived. The prince explained his problem.
'Go and see my uncle, the crow, in the mosque minaret,' she said. 'He knows everything.'

They went to the top of the Seville minaret. The prince explained the problem again – about the princess and the wheat and the eyes like cornflowers. He showed the crow the locket.
'What's her name?' asked the crow.
'I don't know,' said the prince.
'You are in love but you don't know her name?'
'Yes. Is that unusual?'
'Most unusual!' said the crow.

'But if you know everything,' said the prince, 'then you must know what to do.'
'I do know almost everything,' said the crow, 'but I haven't thought about Love for years. Better go to the bird at the foot of the minarets of Cordoba. He knows even more than me. He'll know what to do.'

They travelled to Cordoba and at the foot of the mosque was a parrot. A thousand people were listening to the parrot speak.
'A parrot!' said the prince to the owl. 'Can this be the one?'
'Shh!!' said the parrot's assistant. 'This is Professor Parrot, who is a thousand years old.' The prince waited and waited till the talk was over, then he explained the problem to the parrot.
'Oh!' said the parrot, 'that must be Princess Algeduna. She is locked up by her father and he lets no one see her because he wants to choose her husband when the time is right.'

The parrot flew off to the castle where the princess was held. He perched on a window sill and watched. She was reading a letter and crying.

'I bring you good news,' said the parrot. 'A message from the Prince of Granada.'
'Ahmed!' she cried. 'I have his poems here. They are lovely. How terrible that we shall never meet!'
'Look down there, princess!' said the parrot, pointing with his claw to the street. 'You see that young man with his headscarf on? That's Prince Ahmed.' She smiled from head to toe.
'Tell Ahmed to get ready. Tomorrow I will be seventeen and all my suitors will do battle for me. Give him my scarf and ask him to fight for me.'

How could he fight in the tournament? He had no armour and no horse, no sword! At that moment a large white bird appeared.
'This is Cousin Stork,' said the parrot. 'He will help you.'

Prince Ahmed climbed on the stork's back and they flew to a cave. Inside the cave were a horse and armour and lance and sword. Soon he was ready and rode to the tournament with the princess's scarf around his shoulders. His armour and sword were from a magician and had great power.

'Only until midday,' said the stork, 'will the armour's spell protect you, then you are on your own.'

All morning Ahmed fought and none could defeat him. But the king was unhappy with the thought of a Muslim husband for his daughter and rushed at the prince himself, shouting. The horse shied and knocked the king to the ground.

'Oh no!' thought Ahmed. 'Now I've lost any chance of marrying her!'

He ran back to his cave and returned the next day dressed in rags and sneaked under the princess's window. The princess was sobbing her heart out, thinking she had lost her prince.

Prince Ahmed sang to her – all the poems he had written in his first letter and all those he had imagined since. She sat up and called out for him – 'Where are you?'

'At your feet forever,' he said.

'What's going on?' demanded the king, hearing the noise.

'Only the beginning,' said Ahmed. 'This is a happy beginning which never ends, always coming back from time to time.'

Two birds flew down, picked up the prince and princess and carried them off to the Summer Palace. And there they lived, husband and wife, king and queen, mother and father, delighting in each other's love until the day they died.

10. Jumping Mouse

This is one of the most popular First Nation stories among British storytellers.
It has a marvellous, surprising plot, and a challenging set of learnings.
It can be told quite gently with attention to the voices of the various animals.

Once there was a mouse. He was a busy mouse, doing this and doing that. But every now and then he'd stop and listen. There was a roaring sound somewhere. He wasn't sure if it was in his head or out there in the world.

He asked another mouse, 'Do you hear a roaring in your ears, my brother?'

'No, no,' answered the other mouse, 'I hear nothing. I am busy now. Talk to me later.'

He asked another mouse the same question and the mouse looked at him strangely, 'Are you foolish, mouse? What sound are you on about?'

After that Little Mouse stopped asking but he didn't stop wondering and every now and then he'd stop and listen to the wonderful roaring, always there, quietly as if in the distance.

One day he decided to go off and find where the noise came from. He went off through the long grass in the direction of the sound. It got louder and louder but he still couldn't see what it was. Then someone said, 'Hello!' It was a raccoon. The mouse had never seen one before. Little Mouse was about to scamper off when the raccoon said, 'Don't be frightened. I mean you no harm. Tell me, Little Mouse, what are you doing here all alone?' Little Mouse said, 'I hear a roaring in my ears and I am trying to find out where it comes from.'

'That roaring in your ears,' replied the raccoon, 'is the river.'

'The river?' said the mouse. 'What is a river?'

'Walk with me and I will show you the river,' Raccoon said.

Little Mouse was scared, but he was determined to find out once and for all about the roaring. 'All right, Raccoon, my brother,' said the mouse. 'Lead on to the river. I will walk with you.'

Little Mouse walked with Raccoon. His heart was pounding in his breast. The raccoon took him along many new paths and Little Mouse smelled the scent of many things that he had never smelt before. Finally, they came to the river. It was huge and for the mouse it was amazing. He'd never seen a river before. 'Wow!' Little Mouse said, 'I never imagined anything like this!'

'It is a great thing,' answered the raccoon, 'but here – come and meet my friend.'

In a smoother, shallower place was a lily pad, bright and green. Sitting upon it was a frog – almost as green as the pad it sat on. 'Hello, little brother,' said the frog. 'Welcome to the river.'

'I must leave you now,' said the raccoon, 'but do not fear, little brother. Frog will care for you now.'

'Who are you?' Mouse asked. 'Are you not afraid of being that far out into the great river?'

'No,' answered the frog, 'I am not afraid. I have been given the gift from birth to live both above and in the river. This is my home.'

'Amazing!' said Little Mouse.

'Would you like to know more?' Frog asked.

'Yes please!' said Little Mouse.

'Then try jumping. Jump as high as possible and see what happens.'

Little Mouse started jumping. Every time he jumped he saw the peaks of some beautiful mountains in the distance. He had never seen mountains before but he thought they looked wonderful. 'What are those things up in the sky?' he asked Frog. 'Those are the sacred mountains. Now you have seen them. That is good. Now you can go back to your people with a new name and tell them what you have learned. You are Jumping Mouse.'

Jumping Mouse returned to the world of the mice and tried to tell everyone about his journey and his new name and the river. But no one would listen to him at all. They were busy with food and families and thought him a bit strange. In his mind, Jumping Mouse kept thinking of the beautiful mountains.

The images were deep in his mind and one day he decided to go and climb them. He walked and walked under the cover of the long grass till he came to the foot of the mountains. Here there was no long grass and no bushes for cover. He looked up in the sky and saw eagles circling. He knew they were dangerous. He knew he would be safer hidden in the long grass, but he was determined and he ran off across the bare ground. He ran and he ran, ready at any moment to be caught by an eagle, till he came to a tree. Under the tree the eagles could not see him, so he sat and rested.

He must have fallen asleep because when he woke up there was a buffalo next to him lying on the ground in the shade.
'Hello, my brother,' said the buffalo. 'Thank you for visiting me.'
'Hello, Great Being,' said Jumping Mouse. 'Why are you lying here?'
'I am sick and I am dying,' Buffalo said, 'my eyes are weak and I can see little. Only the eye of a mouse can help me. But I don't know what a mouse is. Do you know?'

Jumping Mouse thought about it. 'He will die,' thought Jumping Mouse, 'if I do not give him my eye. He is too great a being to let die.'
So Jumping Mouse went back to where the buffalo lay and said, 'You, brother,

are a great being. I cannot let you die. I am a mouse and I have two eyes, so you may have one of them.' The minute he said it, Jumping Mouse's eye flew out of his head and the buffalo was healed and could see. He jumped to his feet. 'Thank you, my little brother,' said Buffalo. 'I know of your quest for the sacred mountains and your visit to the river. Now I will protect you. Run under my body as you climb the mountain and you will be safe from the eagles.' They climbed and they climbed with Little Mouse safe under the buffalo's shelter, then the buffalo said, 'Now you must go alone. Goodbye, little friend!'

Jumping Mouse was just looking around when he saw a wolf lying sick on the ground.

'Hello, Brother Wolf,' Jumping Mouse said.

The wolf's ears pricked up and he looked about. 'Oh yes, I am wolf. But not for long. Soon I will die without a mouse's eye.'

Jumping Mouse thought carefully. Could he lose another eye? How would he continue with no eyes? But something inside him said that it was the right thing to do so he said,

'Please take my eye so you can be healed.' As he spoke his eye flew out of his head and the wolf was made whole.

Tears fell down the cheeks of Wolf, but Jumping Mouse could not see them, for now he was blind. 'Thank you, little one,' said the wolf. 'Now let me take you further on your journey. My eyes can be your eyes.'

The wolf guided Jumping Mouse through a pine forest till he came to a lake.

'I must leave you here,' said Wolf.

'Thank you, my brother,' said Jumping Mouse. 'But although I am frightened to be alone, I know you must go.'

Jumping Mouse sat alone there trembling in fear. It was no use running, for he was blind. He knew an eagle could easily catch him now. He felt a shadow on his back and heard the call of an eagle. The next moment he blacked out. Then he found himself up in the air. He opened his eyes and he could see again. He saw the view from high above the earth.

'I can see! I can see!' said Jumping Mouse.

Something flew toward him and said, 'Let the wind carry you, Jumping Mouse. Let it carry you!'

He flew higher and higher, looking down over the mountains and the lake and the wolf, the buffalo, the frog by the river and the mice down in the long grass.

In his mind Jumping Mouse heard Frog's voice saying, 'You have a new name now. You are Eagle.'

11. Jack and Jackie

This Scottish story has the power to get your audience's attention where other stories fail. The shock and curiousness of gender-changing makes the story work easily. If you get a chance, hear the great Ben Haggarty tell this delightful parable about storytelling. It works well if told with glee. It's always fun to imagine gender-swapping – lots of talking points.

Once there was a boy called Jack. Once a month in his town the Lord of the Manor would organise a feast and everyone would be invited. The only thing was, once you were sixteen you had to tell a story or sing a song.

The day after his sixteenth birthday Jack went off to the feast and listened to all the stories as usual, but when it was his turn to tell a story he just went blank.
'I don't know any stories,' he said.
'Well sing us a song!' said the Lord.
'I don't know any songs.'
'Poems?'
'No.'
'Then go down to the river and get us some water to drink.'

Jack slunk out of the room with a bucket and went down to the river. It was icy down there and he slipped on the ice. His feet went up and his head went clunk on the ice. Everything went dark.

When he woke up he felt strange. His body felt different. Rounder. Softer. He felt around under his shirt and… he was a girl! He had all the things that girls had! 'Gosh, what shall I do?' he thought, panicking.

Just then a young man came along and asked Jack if she was OK.
'Yes… er… no,' said Jack, 'I'm a bit cold and lost, can you help?'
'Sure,' said the man, a little flustered. 'What's your name?'
'Er… I don't know. Maybe Jack… or… Jackie!'
'And what are you doing here, Jackie? This is no place for a young woman.'
'I don't know.'
'You don't know? Are you sick?'
'I don't know.'
'So come back to my house. My mum will look after you.'

Jackie walked back, shivering, with the young man and his mum put her to bed with a hot drink. When she woke up they dressed her in a dress and gave her a meal. Jackie stayed there helping around the house and in the kitchen and was soon like one of the family.

A couple of years went by and the man asked her to marry him.
'Yes!' she said, and so they wed.

Soon there was a son and then a daughter and then another son and Jackie loved them more than her own life, cooking and cleaning and taking care of them when they were sick.

Then, one winter evening, she went for a walk with them by the river. One moment she was admiring the view, the next minute she slipped and her feet went up over her head and her head went clunk on the ice. Everything went black.

When she woke up she felt different – stronger, younger. She felt inside her dress and... !!! She was a young man again down by the river with that old bucket. Jack rushed back to the banqueting hall.

'You'll never guess what happened to me!' said Jack as he rushed in.
'Where's the bucket?' asked the Lord of the Manor. 'You had to bring water instead of your story.'
'Forget about that!' said Jack. 'Listen to what happened to me!' And he explained about the ice and everything that happened. Everyone listened, amazed and incredulous.

At the end of the story the Lord laughed. 'Wonderful story, Jack!' he said, patting him on the back. 'You can tell that one as often as you like.'
'But it's true!' said Jack.
'It is truly a great story!' said the Lord. 'And you are a great storyteller!'

And that's how Jack started telling stories.

12. The House That Has Never Known Death

Here's another story about death. There are many versions of this around the world, including the famous Mustard Seed parable of the Buddha. I came across this Saudi version in the amazing Arab Folktales *by Inea Bushnaq.*

Once there was a forest. On the edge of the forest was a village. In the village was a hut and in the hut lived a young couple and their little boy.

Every day the husband would go out hunting in the forest. Every day the little boy would say, 'Daddy! Daddy! Let me come with you!' and every day his mother would say, 'No! He's too young. It's too dangerous.'

Then one time the mother was away and the hunter said, 'OK, son. This time you can come with me.'

They walked into the forest and soon were on the tracks of a gazelle. They came closer and closer until the hunter could see his prey between the trees.
'Just wait here, son, and I'll shoot the gazelle. Then I'll be back.'
'OK, Dad.'

As the little boy waited for his father to return a snake slid out of a tree and bit him on the neck. By the time the father had returned the little boy was dead. The hunter wrapped his son's body in a blanket and carried him home to the village.

When he got back his wife was waiting for him.
'What have you got there?' she asked.

'This is a gazelle that I caught today.'

'Really?' she said. 'Show it to me!'

'There's something I need you to do first, Wife, before I show it to you. I want you to get a cooking pot from another house. A good big one. But it must be from a house that has never known Death. Go around the village and see if you can find me the pot.'

She went to the first house and knocked on the door. A young woman answered.

'Has your house ever known Death?' asked the hunter's wife.

'Yes,' replied the woman. 'About a year ago my father died in this house. I still miss him.'

She went to the second house and again a woman answered.

'Has your house ever known Death?' asked the hunter's wife.

'Yes,' replied the woman. 'My husband died here last year and I am a widow.'

She went to the third house and yet another woman answered the door.

'Has your house ever known Death?'

'Yes,' replied the young woman. 'My baby son died here. It was painful. Even now I grieve.'

The hunter's wife went from house to house and every household had a story of Death. Finally she returned home, her heart full of the tears of every house she had visited.

'I'm sorry, Husband. I've been to every house in the village and in every one I heard a story of Death. Death has come to every house.'

'I know,' said the hunter. 'And now you are ready to see what I have in my blanket. Now it is our turn.'

He showed her their son's body and quietly, together, they prepared for his funeral.

13. Why the Seagull Cries

This is a curious little Raven story from First Nation America. It's full of learnings and levels of meaning. What do we cling to? Why do we suffer? What does it take to let go? All this and more can be found in this tale. Tell it with clarity to the characters of Raven and Seagull, and if you can, practise making a cry like a gull!

In the beginning when the world was new, each animal was given a job. One was in charge of the earth, another in charge of the wind, another in charge of the sea. There was one for clouds and one for rain. The job of looking after light was given to Seagull.

Seagull was so pleased about his job. 'I have the most important job!' he'd brag to the others. 'Without light nothing else can work.'

All of the light in the world was kept in a little box which Seagull looked after, keeping it tightly closed under his wing. He kept it so tightly closed that no light at all could get out. He felt important. He felt good. He felt in control.

The other animals were less happy with the situation. Without light they bumped into each other all the time. Predators couldn't see who to hunt and their prey didn't know who to run from. It was very confusing. There was no light for plants to grow so vegetarians were hungry. Birds flew into trees by mistake. Rabbits went down the wrong rabbit holes. The whole thing was a big mess!

So the animals got together and tried to figure out what to do.

'We have to get Seagull to let out a bit of light from that box!' said Fox.

'I'll talk to him,' said Mouse, who went over and asked very nicely, 'Please, Mr Seagull, would you let some light out of your box? We can't see anything and it's much too dark. Pleeeease!'

Seagull shook his head. 'I'm in charge and I decide what happens to the light. Not you, little mouse!'

Mouse went back and told them what had happened.

Bear got cross. He went over and shouted at Seagull, 'You are not doing your job right! We need the light! Open the box, you foolish bird!'

'If I was so foolish then why have I got such an important job,' pouted Seagull. 'You mind your own business!'

Hyena had a go. He went over and started howling and crying. 'Please, Mr Gull, please give us some light! My family is so hungry. Awww! Awww!'

'Too bad!' said Seagull. 'I'll give you some light when I'm good and ready and not a moment before.'

Animal after animal tried but Seagull would not listen and left them all in the dark. It was looking bad for the world. Life wouldn't last long without light.

Then tricky old Raven croaked up and said, 'I'll sort it out. You leave it to me. Just get me a thorn and I'll sort it.'

Crow brought a long sharp thorn and gave it to Raven, then Raven walked over to Seagull who was strutting on the beach. Raven crept up as silent as a shadow and stuck the thorn into Seagull's foot.

'Aww! Aww! Aww!' cried Seagull. 'Help! Help! My foot hurts!'

'Oh you poor thing!' croaked Raven. 'Let me help you.' He pushed the thorn further into the foot.

'AWW! AWW! AWW! That hurts even more! Why did you do that?'

'Sorry,' said Raven. 'But I couldn't see properly. Could you open your box just a tiny little chink so I can see, then I'll be able to see what I'm doing.'

'OK,' cried Seagull and opened the box so that just a tiny line of light could come out. Raven pushed the thorn in even further.

'AWWWWW! AWWWW! AWWWW! That's even worse! You are hurting me too much!'

'So sorry,' croaked Raven. 'I just need a bit more light. That wasn't enough.' Seagull opened the box a bit more and Raven pushed the thorn really hard.

Seagull was crying now. 'It hurts! It hurts! Please make it stop! Now! Please! Now!'

'Open up the lid so I can see and it'll be fine.'

Seagull was in such pain that he threw the lid right open and out came all the light in a fiery ball and went up into the sky. There was light everywhere but his box was empty.

Raven chuckled, went back to the animals and took a bow. Seagull called after him, 'What about me? What about me?'

'What about you, you stupid bird?' he said and flew off back to the forest. And that is how light came into the world.

Now, even today, you can still hear Seagull cry, because of the pain in his foot, as the thorn is still there.

Seagull also cries with sadness at the loss of his most important job: he was once keeper of the light.

14. Luckily Unlucky

By around ten years of age, children are getting old enough for a little philosophical distance, and here is a great story for that about things not being quite what they seem. Tell it slowly with attention to the character of gossip and the wise granddad. Ensure a knowing narrator's voice.

There was once a village and near that village was a farm. On that farm there lived a farmer, his wife, his mother and father, and his son. One day, the son was out in the fields when he caught a fantastic, wild, white horse. He took it home and all the villagers crowded around.

'Lucky you,' said the villagers, 'to catch such a fantastic horse!'

The son grinned, but his grandfather went over and put his hand on his grandson's shoulder. 'This is maybe not so lucky,' he said. 'Maybe not so lucky.'

The next day the son tried to ride the horse. It jumped and jerked until the son was thrown from its back, breaking the boy's leg in several places. The villagers crowded around as they carried the boy off to the hospital.

'I see what you mean,' said the boy to his granddad, who was walking by the stretcher. 'If I hadn't caught the horse I wouldn't have broken my leg.'

'That was so unlucky,' said the villagers, 'breaking your leg!'
'Maybe not so unlucky. Maybe not unlucky at all,' said Granddad.

A few weeks later war broke out. Soldiers came to the village and rounded up all those who could fight. They did not take the boy with the broken leg.

'I see what you mean,' said the boy to his granddad. 'If my leg wasn't broken I would be sent off to war.'

'Lucky you, not to get taken to war!' said the villagers.
His grandfather stroked his beard. 'Maybe not so lucky,' he said.

A few weeks later a terrible sickness came to the village and many died. The boy was taken to his bed very ill while his granddad watched.

'I see what you mean!' said the boy. 'If I was away at war I wouldn't be sick.'

'Unlucky you, to get sick!' said the villagers.
'Maybe not so unlucky,' said his grandfather.

A nurse came to the house to nurse the boy. They fell in love and in time were married.

At the wedding the boy said to his granddad, 'I see what you mean. If I hadn't been sick I wouldn't have met her.'

'How lucky you were!' everyone said.
And this time his grandfather smiled happily and said nothing.

In time the couple had a baby boy. The baby grew into a fine man. One day, that man was in his field when he caught a fantastic, wild, white horse.

'Lucky you!' said the villagers.
His father stroked his long, white beard. 'Maybe not so lucky,' he thought. 'Maybe not...'

15. Language Lesson

Tell this story if you think your child will get the joke! Build up the tension as the cat approaches and we imagine the worst, then the jump and then the joke.

Once upon a time there was a family of mice living in a nest in a hedge by a field of grass. Every morning they went off to mouse school and studied. They learned about cheese and seeds and nuts and nests and all sorts of things that mice need to know. There were lots of lessons about cats and how cruel they were – how they'd play with little mice for hours just for fun before killing them.

'Keep away from cats!' said their teacher, again and again. 'They are your worst nightmare.' They also had to learn new languages, but they didn't like that much. They'd come back home and moan about the French lessons and the German lessons.

'It's so boring, Mum!' they'd say. 'And what's the point? We just want to live in this little hedge, not travel the world. Why would we want to travel the world? We might meet a cat!'

The mother mouse shook her head. 'It's always good to learn a second language. You never know when it'll come in handy.'

Every afternoon they went out foraging for food, collecting seeds and grains from the fields and woods nearby.

Every evening they heard stories from their gran about the Big Cat who sometimes caught little mice and ate them up.

'If you ever see a cat, or smell a cat, then hide!' she said. 'And if you can't hide then run! And if you can't run then burrow! A cat will eat you up slowly. They are cruel and terrible. There's nothing worse than a cat.'

One such afternoon one of the little mice was eating grain from the top of a stalk of wheat when it saw a big, black cat come slinking across the field towards their nest.

'Oh n-n-n-no!' he squeaked. 'It's a big cat coming this way. It's a cat!'

All the little mice rushed back to their nest deep in the hedge and snuggled up together with their mum, trembling with fear. They imagined being eaten, slowly one by one, bit by bit. Little mouse tears dripped from their eyes.

'Quiet!' whispered their mum. 'He's coming!' The cat was close.

He sniffed around the hedge.

He sniffed around the entrance to the nest.

He pushed his nose into the hedge, slowly, until it was an inch away from their nest with the terrified little mice inside.

He knew there was something there. He wasn't sure what it was.

Maybe a snake that would hurt him? Maybe a rat that would bite him? Maybe something for him to eat?

Cautiously, he waited and watched to see what would happen.

Inside the nest, the mice hearts were beating. They were shaking. They were dead meat. Just then the mother mouse took a deep breath and went, 'WOOF WOOF WOOF WOOF!' as loud as she could.

The cat jumped up and ran off across the field to the other side.

'Wow!' said the little mice. 'Mum! That was amazing!'

'You see, children,' said the mother mouse. 'It is really important to learn a second language. You never know when it might come in handy!'

Nasseradeen Tales

*Nasseradeen is a much loved foolish/wise folk hero
from Iran. His character and stories are popular
throughout the Arab world too, where he usually goes
by the name of Juha, and Hodja in Turkey.
Here are a few samples.*

16. Looking on the Bright Side

Once there was a spate of burglaries in Nasseradeen's street, so Nasseradeen went to bed with a bow and arrow next to his bed, just in case.

One night a noise in the garden disturbed him. He jumped up with his bow and arrow in his hand and looked out of the window. In the garden was a white shape. He couldn't quite see what it was but, just in case it was the burglar, he took a shot at it with his bow and it disappeared. Then he went back to sleep.

The next morning Nasseradeen got up and went out into the garden to see if there was any sign of the burglar. There in the mud, under the washing line, he saw his white nightshirt pinned to the ground with his arrow. He picked them up and started to laugh.

His wife looked out from the window and saw her husband holding his torn gown and the arrow.

'What are you laughing for, you stupid old fool?' she called. 'You've torn your nightgown and it's covered in mud.'

'But wife,' he said, grinning from ear to ear, 'I'm so fortunate. This is such good luck!'

'Why's that?' she asked, curious.

'I'm lucky to have escaped with my life. Imagine what would have happened if I'd been in the nightshirt at the time!'

17. Stop Eating Sweets

Mullah Nasseradeen was known to be good with children. Parents would come to him at the mosque when they had trouble with their kids, and ask for his help.

One day a mother came to him with her young son.

'Tell him to stop eating sweets,' she told Nasseradeen. 'He eats them all the time and they're so bad for his teeth.'

Nasseradeen looked at the boy and was about to speak, when he hesitated.

'Come back in three months,' he said.

The mother obediently took the boy away.

Three months later to the day she came back with her son. Nasseradeen stared severely at the boy. 'Stop eating sweets!' he said.

The mother looked puzzled. 'Why couldn't you have said that three months ago?' she asked.

Nasseradeen smiled sheepishly, 'I had to give up sweets myself first.'

18. Hitting the Target

Once there was a man who wanted to be the best. He didn't mind what he would be the best at, but he wanted to be the best. He chose archery. All day, every day he practised, until every time he shot his arrow he'd hit the bull's-eye. Soon he was champion of his village, then champion of his county and in time he became champion of the country.

Often he'd say to young people, 'If you want to succeed in life then you have to work hard. Practise and practise and that makes perfect. You can do it too. With hard work you can succeed just like me.'

One day, after a competition, a young man approached the archery champion. 'You're very good at archery,' said the man, 'but I know someone who is better than you.'

'Impossible!' said the archer. 'I am the best! On a good day nobody can beat me!'

'I don't agree,' said the young man. 'The one who is better lives over there in that farm. His name is Nasseradeen. If you don't believe me you can go and meet him.'

Together they walked over to the farmhouse, through the gate and into the farmyard. On one side of the yard was a high wooden barn. Painted onto the side of the barn were about a hundred archery targets, circles within circles. Each target had a single arrow stuck exactly at the centre of the bull's-eye.

The archer was impressed. 'Wow!' he thought, 'I can hit the bull's-eye, but he can hit the exact centre of the bull's-eye. That's amazing!'

Nasseradeen came out to say hello.

'Tell me,' said the archer, 'I've practised my whole life to be as good as I can. I can hit the bull's-eye every time, but you not only hit the bull's-eye, you get it right in the very, very centre. How do you do that?'

Nasseradeen smiled. 'Well, you do things your way,' he said, 'and I do things my way. You see, me, first I shoot the arrow, then I paint the target around it!'

19. Nasseradeen and the Perfect Wife

One New Year's Eve Nasseradeen was sitting with a friend drinking coffee and mulling over their plans for the coming year.

'Friend,' Nasseradeen said. 'I think it's time I found a wife. This single life is getting tiresome. It's time I found a good woman to share my life with.'

'Good idea!' said his friend. 'But a good woman is hard to find. What kind of wife would you like?'

'Oh I know exactly what kind of woman I want,' he said. 'She will have to be beautiful, cultured and spiritually developed. That would make her the perfect wife.'

'Good luck, my friend.'

The year went by and on New Year's Eve the two friends met again.

'So tell me, how did you get on with your search for your perfect wife?'

'Not too well,' said Nasseradeen. 'I found someone who was really beautiful. She had a lovely face, lovely hair, lovely skin, lovely everything... the most beautiful woman I've ever seen. I think she liked me, but the trouble was that she had never read a book and knew nothing about music or poetry, so she just wasn't for me. She had no culture. Next year I'll look further afield.'

'Good luck, my friend.'

The year went by and on New Year's Eve the two friends met again.

'So tell me, how did you get on with your search for your perfect wife?'

'I looked in all the towns in this part of the country till I found this gorgeous woman, as lovely as I could have dreamed of, and so cultured. We had read all the same books and poets and we talked for hours about music and poetry. She was perfect, except ... well, she never went to the mosque and knew nothing of the holy books. So of course she wasn't for me. Next year I'll have to try even further afield.'

The year went by and on New Year's Eve the two friends met again.

'And how did you get on this year?' asked his friend. 'Did you finally find your perfect wife?'

'I did,' replied Nasseradeen, smiling. 'She was absolutely perfect. She was drop-dead gorgeous, totally cultured and passionate about religion. She went to the mosque every day and knew all the Koran by heart. She was perfect.'

'Congratulations,' said his friend. 'So have you got married yet?'

'No,' said Nasseradeen shaking his head. 'There was just one problem ... she was looking for the perfect husband!'

20. The Neighbour's Cockerel

Nasseradeen lived next to a farm. One time his neighbour got a new cockerel which liked to crow in the middle of the night.

Nasseradeen would be fast asleep when the animal would call: COCKADOODDLE DOO!

After that Nasseradeen couldn't get back to sleep. He'd lie awake fuming. Every day he moaned to his wife over breakfast.

'That cockerel is so annoying. That farmer is such a bad neighbour. He should keep that animal quiet!'

'Oh you poor thing!' she'd say. 'But what can you do? Our neighbours are farmers and they need a cockerel.'

After a few weeks Nasseradeen had had enough.

'Wife!' he fumed. 'I'm going round to our neighbours to sort out this cockerel thing once and for all.'

He stormed off to the neighbour's house while his wife waited worrying in case there would be trouble.

An hour later Nasseradeen came back holding the offending cockerel.

'What have you done?' she asked.

'I bought the cockerel off the farmer,' he told her. 'Now we'll see how he likes it when my cockerel wakes him up in the middle of the night!'

21. Nasseradeen's Nail

Nasseradeen lived in a fine big house while his neighbour lived in a smaller one. The neighbour was jealous. One day he decided to try and persuade Nasseradeen to sell his house by making his life miserable.

First he got up every night and made as much noise as possible, banging pots and pans and singing at the top of his voice. When Nasseradeen asked him to stop he said, 'No, I can't stop, but if you would like to sell your house then I'd be happy to buy it.'

'Really?' said Nasseradeen. 'I'll think about it.'

Next, as well as the noise every night, rubbish started appearing in Nasseradeen's garden every morning. He knew it was from his neighbour.

'Do you know anything about all that rubbish in my front garden?' Nasseradeen asked his neighbour.

'Oh, the neighbourhood is going downhill, I suppose. It's a good time to sell up and leave, don't you think?'

The last straw came when Nasseradeen was walking past his neighbour's house one day. His neighbour threw a bucket of dirty water out of the doorway, right onto Nasseradeen's head.

'Oops,' said the neighbour. 'Didn't see you there!'

Nasseradeen said nothing and went home to change.

The next day he went to visit his neighbour and told him he was ready to sell.

'How much will you give me for my house?' asked Nasseradeen.

'Twenty thousand dinars,' replied the neighbour, very pleased that his plan had worked.

'Fine,' replied Nasseradeen, 'I'll sell it to you for half, for ten thousand dinars.'
'Why?' asked the astonished neighbour.
'Well, the thing is, there is the matter of my nail. You see in the house there is a nail. It belonged to my father and before that to his father and I am very fond of it. I am willing to sell you my house, but on the condition that I keep the nail. It's stuck in the wall in the front room. I want to be able to visit the nail whenever I want, and hang whatever I want on it, to honour the memory of my father and grandfather. Agree to that and I'll give you the house for half price.'

The neighbour couldn't believe his luck, getting the house and for half price! So he readily agreed. Lawyers were brought in, signing over the house, but giving Nasseradeen rights to his nail.

The next evening, the neighbour was fast asleep in his new home, when a knock came on the door. It was Nasseradeen, come to visit his nail. Well, it was a nuisance, but for 10,000 dinars saved, it was worth it. The neighbour went back to bed, and Nasseradeen went to his nail.

In the morning the neighbour woke to a disgusting smell. He and his wife went downstairs and found, hanging on the nail, a pair of rotten old boots, smelling like a rubbish dump and teeming with maggots and slugs. The smell was terrible throughout the house, but well, for ten thousand dinars they would put up with it.

A few nights later there was another midnight knock on the door – Nasseradeen again.
'Oh thank God you're back!' said the neighbour. 'Please take away the boots!'
'Yes, I'm planning to take them away,' said Nasseradeen, shuffling towards his nail.
'Good!' said the neighbour and went back to bed.

The next morning the neighbour woke up itching all over. His body was covered in little insect bites which itched like mad. His wife and kids were also covered in bites. They looked around for the source and found an old jacket hanging up on Nasseradeen's nail. The jacket was actually light green, but it was covered in so many fleas that from a distance it seemed black. The fleas were hungry and jumped at any warm-blooded creature they could find. Nasseradeen's neighbour washed and scrubbed the house all day, but more and more fleas kept jumping off the coat, keeping his whole family awake every night for a week.

Finally a knock on the door came in the middle of the night. 'Please! Please!' begged the neighbour, 'Please take away that jacket! It's driving me mad!'
'Oh, I am sorry to hear that,' replied Nasseradeen with a smile. 'You'll be pleased to hear I'm going to take it away.'

Nasseradeen went to his nail and replaced the coat with two rotten old fish. If the boots had smelt bad, the fish were a hundred times worse. Everything in the house smelt of rotten fish, the kids smelt so bad they were sent home from school, and the neighbour smelt so bad nobody would buy from his shop...

The neighbour had had enough – he went off to find Nasseradeen.

'Please,' he begged. 'Buy your house back. It's unbearable for us to live there with that nail of yours. Please take it back!'

And so Nasseradeen bought his house back for half the price he had been paid for it, and his neighbour never tried to get rid of him again...

22. Nasseradeen and the King's Hunting Party

Once, the king was out hunting in the forest when he saw Nasseradeen by the side of the road.

'Not you!' shouted the king. 'You always bring me bad luck. If I see you before hunting then I won't catch anything. Guards! Beat this man severely and order him to keep out of my way!'

So the king's soldiers whipped, punched and kicked Nasseradeen, and left him lying unconscious in a pool of blood.

It turned out that the hunting went well and the king rode triumphant back towards the palace.

On the road he met Nasseradeen, hobbling back home with several broken ribs, two black eyes and aching limbs.

'Ah, Nasseradeen,' said the king magnanimously, 'How are you doing?'

'Aching, your majesty, aching.'

'Oh yes,' said the king generously, 'Sorry about that! The thing is, when I saw you I thought you were bad luck'.

'Really, your majesty? YOU thought I was bad luck!'...

23. Nasseradeen Speaks Truth

Once Nasseradeen was advisor to the king. One day Nasseradeen advised the king that truth was the highest good that all should seek with vigilance and determination. The king was persuaded, and was determined to do something about it. He issued a declaration that all his people must tell the truth from now on. Anyone caught lying would be hanged. He told his guards at the gates of the city that they should question everyone entering the gates. Those that told the truth should be allowed to pass, those that lied should be taken and hanged.

The next day Nasseradeen was entering the city when a guard stopped him.
'Where are you going?' asked the guard.
'To be hanged!' replied Nasseradeen grimly.
'Is that the truth?' asked the guard.
'You tell me,' replied Nasseradeen.

Well the guard tried to puzzle it out. He thought, 'If I take him and hang him then he will have told the truth so I can't hang him, but if I don't hang him then he will have been lying so he should have been hanged...'?

The guard couldn't decide so he took Nasseradeen to see the king. The king looked displeased. 'What are you up to?' he said.
'Are you going to hang me or not?'
'If I hang you then you would have been telling the truth. If I don't hang you then you would have been lying.'

'Do you now see, your majesty, what you mean when you talk about truth? You mean your truth. Here there are three truths, yours, mine and the guard's.'

The king laughed and cancelled his decree.

24. Nasseradeen and the Light

One time Nasseradeen was kneeling on the ground under a street light. His friend came over and Nasseradeen told him he was looking for his keys, so his friend knelt down under the light and helped with the search.

After a while the friend asked, 'Where did you drop the keys, Nasseradeen?'

'I dropped them over there,' replied Nasseradeen, pointing to a dark corner away from the light.

'So why are we searching over here?' asked the friend.

'It's much too dark to see anything over there,' replied Nasseradeen. 'Over here there's plenty of light so I'm searching here!'

25. Nasseradeen Teaches Justice

Nasseradeen was asked to solve a dispute between two brothers who had inherited their family's land and gold, amounting to more than 1,000 gold dinars. They couldn't agree on how it should be divided. Nasseradeen agreed to mediate, on the condition that his decision was binding on both sides. The brothers agreed, trusting in his wisdom.

'The main question,' said Nasseradeen, 'is whether you want human justice or divine justice.'

The brothers were devout believers and agreed that they wanted divine justice.

'OK,' said Nasseradeen. 'The older brother gets two chickens and a donkey, the younger gets the land, the gold and everything else.'

'Why!' complained the older. 'That's not fair!'

'Do you think it is more fair, the way that God has organised the world?' replied Nasseradeen.

26. Who Do You Trust?

Nasseradeen's neighbour was always trying to borrow things from Nasseradeen. One time he came round and knocked on Nasseradeen's door.

'I need to borrow your donkey,' he announced. 'Mine is too tired for ploughing, so will you lend me yours?'

'I'm sorry, neighbour,' said Nasseradeen, 'I would lend you my donkey, but he's not here.' As chance would have it, as Nasseradeen was speaking a loud EE-AWW came from behind the house where Nasseradeen's stables were. Obviously it was his donkey.

'But Nasseradeen,' complained his neighbour, 'Your donkey is in the stables, I just heard him.'

'Impossible!' said Nasseradeen confidently. 'The donkey is not there. I told you.'

But again, as he was speaking the sound of a braying donkey was heard from behind the house.

'Nasseradeen, I just heard the donkey!' argued the neighbour, firmly.

'No, you didn't. It must have been a dog barking.'

Just then the EE-AAW came for a third time from behind the house.

'There it is again, Nasseradeen. You can't deny that was your donkey!' Nasseradeen paused for thought and gave his beard a stroke.

'It seems to me,' he said, 'that this is a question of trust. Who do you trust? Do you trust me, or do you trust the donkey?'

27. Nasseradeen and the Turnips

One time Nasseradeen had a good crop of turnips, each one the size of a large watermelon. He decided to give a sack of his turnips to the king to celebrate the fine harvest. Walking along the road to the palace a friend asked him where he was going, and Nasseradeen explained he was taking the turnips as a gift for the king.

'You can't give the king turnips!' protested the friend. 'They are not suitable at all. You should give him a fine, sweet fruit. Here, give me the turnips and take this plate of figs!'

So Nasseradeen took the figs to the king and handed him the plate. Now it happened that the king was in a bad mood that day, and as soon as he got the plate he started throwing the figs at Nasseradeen. To the king's surprise, Nasseradeen waved his hands towards the sky, laughing and shouting, 'Thanks to God for the figs! Thanks to God for the figs!'

The king was curious. 'Nasseradeen, why are you laughing and shouting?'

'Well you see, your majesty, I was going to bring turnips but my friend told me to bring figs. If you had thrown turnips at me, I would be dead by now!'

28. Cause and Effect

Nasseradeen was sprinkling sawdust in his garden when his neighbour poked his nose over the fence and asked Nasseradeen why he was sprinkling sawdust.

'I'm sprinkling sawdust to keep away the tigers!' replied Nasseradeen.

'But there aren't any tigers in this country!' answered the puzzled neighbour. Nasseradeen smiled: 'Well, that just proves how well it's working!'

29. Nasseradeen Teaches Empathy

One time Nasseradeen was walking along a long road with his disciple beside him. Suddenly a great wagon came roaring along the road drawn by six great horses. The driver was in a terrific hurry, and shouted at Nasseradeen and his companion to get out of the way. Unfortunately they didn't move in time, and both men were knocked into a rather muddy drainage ditch by the side of the road.

Nasseradeen stood up and waved his fist at the departing wagon.

'May all your needs be satisfied!' he shouted after the wagon.

His disciple was puzzled. 'Why did you say that, Nasseradeen? He could have killed us!'

'That's true,' answered Nasseradeen. 'But do you think that he would have knocked us into the ditch if all his needs had been satisfied?'

30. Children of Wax

This is a frequently told African story about children made out of wax who can't go out in the day. Evoke the worry of the parents and the trapped feeling of the child who wants to explore. Let the tragedy of the melting sink in before moving to the final transformation scene. As your child prepares to leave for a new school this can be a great transition story.

Once there was a forest where the sun blazed fiery and hot every day of the year. In the middle of the forest was a village of thatched huts, where the hunters hunted and the farmers farmed and the children played in the sun. Some played football, some played tag, and some went exploring in the forest.

One day a hunter got married and built a hut from wood and leaves on the edge of the village where he lived with his wife. Soon her belly swelled and she gave birth to a lovely baby boy.

The midwife was there at the birth. She looked at the baby boy and frowned. 'This is no ordinary child,' she said. 'He is not made of flesh, he is made of wax. You will have to keep him indoors. If he goes into the sun then he will melt.'

Two other children were born, a boy and a girl, and they too were made of wax. All three were kept indoors until night-time when they were allowed out – but not far. It was dangerous to go out of the village at night so they had to stay close to the hut in case lions or tigers were out hunting, or in case they trod on a snake.

In the day their mother would sit with them and tell them stories about the wide world. Mountains, oceans, deserts and forests. Tales of adventure and amazing creatures.

The eldest son was restless. Every day he'd peep through the cracks in the wall at the world outside. He wanted so badly to go out and explore the forest, travel to the ocean, climb the mountain. He looked up at the birds in the sky and envied them.

As he watched, he sang this song:

> *I want to break free*
> *Go out of these walls*
> *To climb many mountains and sail seven seas.*
> *I want to be free*
> *To go my own way*
> *Not stuck inside*
> *These old cold walls.*

'No!' said his mother. 'You cannot leave! You will melt in a moment.'

One day he'd had enough. He pushed open the door and ran out into the sunlight. His brothers watched as he stood there in the sun, staring up at the sky. He sang his song and danced in the dust. In a few moments his head began to melt, then his arms and his chest, and finally his legs, till there was just a puddle of wax on the ground. When night fell the children went outside and scooped up all the wax.

'He loved birds,' said his sister, 'let's make him into a bird.'

They moulded the wax into the shape of a bird and covered it in cool green leaves to protect it from the sun, then left it perching on the fence outside their hut.

The next morning at dawn they watched through the window, wondering if the bird would melt. But something else happened. As they watched the leaves seemed to turn into feathers, the wax eyes turned into living beady eyes, the waxy beak into a sharp black beak. The bird opened its wings and glided up on an updraft high above the hut, circling and calling down. His brother and sister thought they could hear the same song:

> *Now I've broken free*
> *Gone out of these walls*
> *Now I'll climb many mountains and see seven seas.*
> *I will be free*
> *To go my own way*
> *Not stuck inside*
> *These old cold walls.*

They watched, delighted, as he flew away toward the mountain, which rose high and mighty above the forest.

31. Warrior

This story, sometimes called the Black Prince, is both memorable and powerful, evoking the tragedy of a young man who feels he is not good enough, not likeable, and so misses his chance for happiness. This story works well with 8–11 year olds, encouraging the idea of taking the opportunities which life offers, and overcoming the fears which hold us back. If you can play a flute or recorder, even just a little, use it in the story. It's one of my favourites. For a change here's a long text with lots of things you can include. For a shorter text you can use Laura Simm's version in Holt's Ready-To-Tell Tales.

Once there was a desert. In that desert there was a city built from bricks the colour of red blood. In that city there was a boy. His name was Kassim.

On the day of his birth his mother looked at him and thought he looked odd, strange, ugly even. As if there were two faces pressed together into one. At school they bullied him for looking different, and at home his siblings shunned him. Kassim grew up lonely and alone, with just one thing that brought him joy. His father had given him a flute, and when he felt unhappy he'd close his eyes and play his flute. It took him to a place of freedom and peace.

Our story begins with Kassim as a young man walking through the city when he saw a white wall in the distance: in that city of red walls, there was something white! He went to the wall – it was so white and cool – and then climbed a tree so he could peep over the top. Inside was a garden: crammed with colour and filled with fragrance. At the centre was a young woman sitting by a lotus pool.

Kassim found her lovely. He wanted to call out and make friends but, before he could speak, a voice inside him said, 'No she would not want to see you. You are ugly'.

So he kept quiet and just watched her, then climbed down from the tree, sat there with his eyes closed, and played his flute.

The next day he came back and climbed the tree again. She was there but he couldn't find the courage to speak. That same inner voice said 'No!'. Then he climbed down, closed his eyes, and played his flute, then went off home.

This went on for 100 days: for 100 days he visited, couldn't find the courage to speak, and then played his flute before leaving.

Then on the hundreth day he was in the market and overheard some old ladies talking:
'That princess, she just spends all her time in the white walled garden!' said one.
'I know,' said the other. 'About time she got married I'd say!'

Kassim realised the girl he had been watching was the daughter of the king, the richest man in the city, and Kassim was from the poorest of families. Now he was sure they would never be friends. That day he walked around the city fed up and frustrated. Around dusk he saw a fire in the desert and left the city to find it. There was a circle of travellers sipping coffee and swapping stories. He listened to the tales, and when it was his turn he told his own story, about school and home, and then about the garden and the girl.

'I just wish I could be someone else' he said, 'then things would be OK.'

A man in a green robe stood up across the fire.

'There is a man who can change you, just once, into something else. Would you like that?'

Kassim nodded.

The next day Kassim and the green man travelled out into the desert to an oasis, where the wizard waited.

When they arrived Kassim asked, 'Will you change me?'
'What into?' asked the wizard.
'Someone strong, handsome and a good fighter?'
'OK, but you know I can't change you back if you change your mind. Anyway what will you give me?'

Kassim handed over his flute and the deal was done.

Three months later war broke out in the desert. Invaders came from the mountains and did battle with the soldiers from the Red City, but the invaders were stronger. Soon the city would fall: the king's head would be on a spike and his family slaves.

On that day a stranger came to the city: tall, strong, in the armour of a warrior and with a strong handsome face. He went to the king:

'Let me lead your army, and we will win' he said.

The king, with nothing to lose, agreed. And with the warrior in the lead, the invaders were driven away within a week.

The king organised a feast to honour the warrior. At the high table of honour there was the king, his daughter and the stranger.

In his speech he said:

'Let him name his reward. If I can grant it I will do so. I owe him my life.'

The warrior stood. 'Let me marry your daughter,' he said simply. The princess looked at him.

'I will marry you if you wish' she said, 'as you have saved us all, but first hear my story.'

'A few months ago I was sitting in my garden when I heard a flute being played. The music was so beautiful, and I had to know who was playing. I climbed a tree and peeped over the wall and there was a young man... with the most lovely face I had ever seen. Like summer and winter in one place, lovely. I wanted to call out and say hello, but couldn't find the courage. I just climbed down and waited, listening, hoping he would come and say hello. But the music stopped and he went away.

'The next day I waited in the garden and heard the music again. Again I peeped over the wall and there he was but I couldn't find the courage to speak.

'This went on for 100 days, then he stopped coming. I don't know why, but the truth is that I want to touch his face, hear his music. I will marry you if you like, but it is him I long for.'

The warrior stared at his feet for a while.

'I once had a dream like your dream,' he said. 'My dream is gone now. I would not take your dream away from you.'

He walked out into the desert and was never seen in the Red City again. When he died he asked that this be written on his grave:

> *Three things in life cannot be taken back: an arrow from a bow,*
> *words from the mouth, or a missed opportunity.*

32. Baldur

This is a great story from the Norse myths. Before you start, explain the main gods (Odin, Frigga, Baldur, Hodur and Loki) so your child gets used to their names. Evoke the beauty of Baldur and how loved he is, the jealous trickiness of Loki, and the grief of his mother.

Once, Odin's wife, Frigga, gave birth to a son called Baldur. Baldur was the most lovely and handsome of all the gods and the best loved. He ruled over light and spring, all things right and good and he was loved by all, or almost all.

Then one night his mother had a dream. Baldur was in the underworld with the Goddess Hel, its ruler. Baldur was dead. His mother was troubled by the dream and told it to her husband.

Odin went to the grave of Wala, one who could see the future, and summoned her from her grave. 'Tell me,' he said, 'who will be the next to go to the realm of Hel?'

'It will be Baldur,' she crooned. 'And the cause will be his blind brother, Hodur.'

Immediately the gods all met to decide what to do. They agreed that every creature on earth would swear an oath never to harm Baldur. In this way he could not be killed. This was their plan.

Frigga, his mother, organised the swearing. The sky, the earth, fire, water, giants, dwarves, elves and men as well as every plant and animal in the world swore their oath never to hurt Baldur.

From that moment on nothing could hurt the beautiful young god. Rocks did not bother him, arrows could not pierce him, swords just bounced from his skin. The beautiful young god was invincible. The gods were so happy that they started playing a game. Who could kill Baldur? Nobody! Baldur stood and they would all attack him, laughing, with spears, arrows, swords and knives. Nothing could hurt him. Everyone was delighted with the game.

Well, almost everyone. Loki, the trickster, had other ideas. Loki knew that on an old oak tree there was a plant – mistletoe – which had not sworn the oath to protect Baldur. It seemed so harmless that Frigga had not bothered with the oath. Loki cut a twig from the mistletoe, then he returned to the circle of the gods. They were still playing their weapons game with Baldur. The only one standing aside was the blind Hodur.

'How can I play when I can't see what I'm doing?' he complained to Loki.

'Take your bow and get ready to shoot,' replied Loki, 'and here is your arrow.' He handed Hodur the twig. 'I'll help you aim,' he said.

Hodur shot the mistletoe twig and it pierced Baldur's side. He fell to the ground and, as his parents held him in their arms, he died.

So the gods set about burying the body of their beloved Baldur. They erected a funeral pyre on Baldur's own ship, Ringhorn. At the sight of her much loved husband, dead upon the pyre, Nanna, his widow, died of a broken heart. Her body was laid at the side of her husband's.

The giants pushed the burning ship out into the open waters and wild flames accompanied the god on his last journey. When the ship finally sank into the depth of the ocean, it seemed as if the whole world went into a grieving twilight.

No one was grieving more than Frigga, his mother. Was Baldur, the God of Light and Springtime, lost forever? Was there a way she could persuade Hel, the goddess who ruled in the land of the dead, to let Baldur return to the daylight?

Touched deeply by Frigga's grief, Hermodur, the messenger god, decided to try and free his brother. For nine nights, Hermodur rode his father's eight-legged horse down to the underworld until he reached Bifröst, the bridge that separates the world of the dead from the world of the living. He crossed over the bridge and found Baldur, pale and dazed. He called to Hel, asking her to release him but she shook her head. 'The dead are for my realm alone, Baldur belongs to me.'

'But all the world is grieving. Every creature in the world is crying for him.'

'I don't think so!' replied Hel scoffing.

'It is so,' said Hermodur.

'If all creatures will cry for him, then I will let him go!' she said. Hermodur returned to the gods and told his story.

Frigga sent out the elves to ask that all things in the world should cry for Baldur.

The stones cried, the sky cried, the earth cried, the sea cried, animals wept and plants sobbed. Things were looking quite good for Baldur until the elves found a cave with a giantess in it.

'Cry for Baldur!' they asked, but she shook her head.

'Please!' they begged but she would not.

Some say that she was Loki in disguise. Who knows?

What is known is that, without her tears, Baldur was stuck in the underworld with Hel, which suited her just fine.

As for clever tricky Loki, the gods sent the giants to catch him.

He had just finished making a net for fishing. When the giants came he threw the net in the fire, burning it, jumped into a stream and swam away to the sea. But the gods saw the shape of the net in the ashes and made a net just like it. They waited by the river for their chance. When he swam upstream they caught him and punished him.

He was taken to an island in the realm of Hel and bound to a sharp-edged rock. Above his head they hung a huge black snake, who continuously dripped acid poison into his face, burning him horribly. Sigyn, his wife, came to him and held the bowl above his head to catch the acid, but every time she went away to empty the bowl he was burned again by the poison. He screamed and trembled and the earth shook. This is the true source of earthquakes.

So it is and so it will remain until the end of all things.

33. Ericython

This story, from Ancient Rome, is all about respect for a forest. When a king cuts it down he is cursed by its guardian and pays a terrible price. It can be seen as a story about what happens if we do not respect the environment. It's quite a gory and shocking tale, which is usually popular with this age group. I like Ted Hughes's version in his Tales from Ovid.

Once there was a greedy king called Ericython.
He loved money more than anything, more even than the gods.

One day he decided that a grove of oak trees should be cut down for wood and sold. These trees belonged to Ceres, Goddess of Life. It was forbidden to cut any of her trees, but Ericython didn't care.

He took his woodcutters to the grove and ordered them to chop the trees down, but nobody moved.

'We dare not!' said the chief woodcutter. 'These are sacred trees. The gods will punish us if we harm them.'

'If you don't,' snarled the king, 'then I will punish you! These trees are worth good money. Cut them down or I will cut you down.'

Reluctantly, the men began to work. As their axes cut into the trees, red sap sprayed out, as if the trees were bleeding.

They chopped down every tree and loaded the wood on carts for sale in the town.

From the heavens, Ceres was watching.

Cold and furious, she pondered a suitable punishment for this greedy stupid king. She called to the God of Hunger, who lived in the land of ice and snow in the far north. When Hunger heard the call she was scratching lichen and moss from a rock to eat. Her head was like a skull, her skin so thin that the bones beneath could all be seen. Her teeth were broken and bloody. Her organs could be seen through her skin – tiny belly and guts, heart and lungs. No fat, no meat, just skin and bone.

She jumped onto the wind and floated easily south until she came to Ericython's house, floating in through the window of the bedroom where he slept.

For a while she crouched over his snoring body and then clamped her bony mouth to his fat lips. She breathed ice cold hunger into his mouth then floated away.

In the morning he woke, ready for breakfast. He ate and ate but the more he ate the more he wanted. All morning he ate breakfasts, then lunches and dinners, but seemed to ache with hunger all the time. He couldn't sleep. His hunger was too much. He just sat in the kitchen eating and eating, day and night.

Soon the food in the house was all gone, and he ordered his servants to sell whatever they needed so they could keep buying food. Within a month his savings were gone. Within a year everything in the palace was sold. It was empty, with all the servants gone: just him and his daughter.

He took her to the slave market and sold her as a slave to buy food.

Finally, when he had nothing left to sell, he sat in the street and started to feed on his own fingers. When they were gone he ate his toes, then started biting and swallowing the flesh from his own arms and legs, until there was nothing left but a head and limbless body, dead in a pool of blood.

This was the revenge of Ceres.

34. Quetzalcoatl Brings Chocolate to Earth

This is an Aztec story of creation, the fall from grace of the creator, and his parting gift to the world: chocolate! It is an extraordinary tale with echoes of Prometheus and Osiris, featuring drunkenness as a route to doom.
It is a creation story, so tell it with atmosphere and spaciousness.

In the beginning there was no life on this earth. Just rock and sky. Black, bare rock. Clear wide sky. Just that...

Then the Dragon God Quetzalcoatl woke up. Up in the heavens in his cloud cave, the Dragon God stretched, yawned and looked over the edge of the earth down onto the bare black rock of earth.

'I can do better,' he thought. 'This place needs some life.'

He filled his dragon lungs and breathed down onto the earth:
Sea... he breathed and the sea became.
Forest... he breathed and forest became.
Moorland... Desert... Lion... etc.

All day he breathed life onto the earth and then, pleased with his work, he slept. The next day he woke and looked down again at the earth now teeming with life. 'Hmm,' he thought, 'just one more thing.'

He slipped out of his cave, stretched his wings and flew up to perch on the morning star. He waited until a ray of light shone down onto the earth and hooking his tail around the light he slid down towards earth.

As his claws touched the ground, he transformed into a man with thick strong fingers, a smile on his face and a jaunty hat on his head. He walked over to a field of corn, picked some cobs, and then ground the corn into flour between two stones. Next, he mixed in water and shaped the dough into two figures, one man and one woman. When that was done he leaned down over the figures and breathed on them... Live... and they transformed into four men and women. Breathing and hearts pumping.

He turned to the ray of starlight – as his hand touched the light he returned to his dragon form, hooked his tail around the light, opened his wings and followed the light back up to the morning star.

The people watched.
'Who was that?' said one.
'That was our father, our maker, our God,' said another.
'Then we must worship him every day,' said a third.
'Let's start now,' said a fourth.
They sang and danced for the dragon, and he heard the sound and was pleased.

Time passed and every day Quetzalcoatl worked in the heavens to the sound of their singing and their praises. Every morning he smiled, yawned and purred as he watched his people honour him before starting their day.
'It is good,' he purred.

Then one day there was silence when he woke. He looked down and saw that the people had made statues of all kinds of creatures and were worshiping them instead. 'Time I paid them a visit,' he thought, perched on the morning star, and slid down the starlight ray to earth.

As he came down people stopped and stared – 'Who's that?'

'It's a dragon,' said one.

'I remember the story,' said another.

'It's our father, our maker, come back to visit,' said a third.

When Quetzalcoatl's claws touched the ground he turned into a man with thick hands, a big smile and a jaunty hat.

'Do you know me?' he asked.

'Yes. You are our father,' they said.

'Good!' he said.

'Wait!' they said.

They took sticks and broke apart the clay gods they had made.

'Now we will worship you!'

They built him a temple with four stone pillars in the shape of men, holding up the roof with their hands. Outside were carvings of tigers and butterflies. Inside was a throne for Quetzalcoatl.

Every day he sat and the people came and sang him their song of praise, dancing for their father. Every day he smiled and said, 'Now, let me teach you something.'

On the first day he taught them fire.

On the second how to plough and sow, and water and harvest.

On the third day he taught them to grind and bake.

On the fourth day he taught them to build.

On the fifth day to play music.

On the sixth day to count and multiply.

On the seventh day to write and read.

Week by week they listened and learned and soon their city was growing into a great and happy place – food, shelter, arts flourished under Quetzalcoatl's guidance. Quetzalcoatl sat happily on his throne and watched, pleased that his people were happy. Then he thought,

'We need just one more thing to make life even sweeter. Then this would be perfect.' He went to the morning starlight, turned into a dragon and flew up to the heavens.

There he saw a crowd of gods drinking from golden goblets and behind them the fields of bushes where they grew the beans to make the drink. As the gods chatted and sipped he sneaked over to the field, gently pulled up one of the bushes, slipped it under his feathered wing, and went back unseen to earth.

There he went to a farmer and planted a field of cuttings from the bush. He helped the farmer water them, and watched as they flowered in spring, gave red fruits in summer, which dried to dry brown beans in autumn. Then he showed the farmer how to pick and roast and grind the beans, then mix them with water to drink.

The farmer added some honey and chilli and gave the drink to the king. He sipped it and felt his body fill with happiness.

'Good!' he said. 'This is a drink fit for the gods. Now it will be the drink of kings.'

Every day the royal family supped at the sweet drink and were content. Then one day the God of Darkness looked down from the heavens and saw the kings drinking. He called out to the other gods:

'Look! See what Quetzalcoatl has done. He has given our drink to them. He is a thief. I will punish him!'
'Yes!' they said. 'Punish him well!'

Turning into a huge spider he hooked his thread onto the edge of heaven and lowered himself down to earth. As he touched the ground he turned into the form of a thin man with long thin hands, a bitter smile and a thin dark hat on his very thin head.

He went to Quetzalcoatl in the temple with a large pot of something.'Quetzalcoatl,' he said, 'I come from heaven. I have something for you that all the gods are drinking all the time. It's the best drink there is. Better than that old drink of the gods. Its happiness is stronger. Try it!'

Quetzalcoatl was curious and drank from the pot. It was curious. A bit bitter, but he felt himself relax as he drank. It was beer.

Soon his head was spinning. He tried to walk but kept on falling over.
'What's happening?' said the people.

He started to laugh and laugh in a strange way.
'What's going on?' said the people.

He jumped around singing and doing a drunken dance.
'This is not right!' said the people.

He got angry and started shouting and smashing things.
'This is not worthy of respect!' said the people.
'Who wants to fight?' he shouted, and the people turned their backs on him.
'We will not worship you anymore,' they said.

In the morning he had a headache. He saw the people looking for new gods and he felt shame. He walked away from his people and he saw that the fields where the beans had been grown had changed. Now the bushes grew the fruit for the beer he had drunk. The place was no longer perfect.

He walked away until he came to the sea. By the beach was a field. He reached into his pocket and pressed three beans into the soil, then, touching a ray of sunlight he turned into a dragon and flew away from the earth forever.

When the seeds sprouted to bushes and flowers became fruits and dry beans, a farmer took the beans and made them into a drink.

'This is good!' said his wife as she sipped. 'What is it?'
'This is the drink of the gods,' said the farmer. 'Chocolate!'

35. Skeleton Woman

Skeleton Woman is a very popular Inuit story made famous by the landmark book,
Women Who Run with the Wolves by C.P. Estes. I have found that this story
works well with 10–11 year olds, mixing the spookiness of a weird ghost story with
the mythology of rebirth as a skeleton reclaims her body and her life. Create an
atmosphere of mystery and fear for the fisherman, then tenderness in the final scene.

Father and daughter stand on the top of the cliff. Beneath them the water breaks on the rocks. The father's eyes are angry. He holds his daughter's neck. Her eyes wide with fear. Shouting at her. She screams.

Maybe she was pushed, who knows? Maybe she slipped. Whatever the cause, she fell, her body twisting and turning as she fell through the air, crashing and cracking against the rocks like a limp, lifeless puppet, breaking her neck on the rocks below.

The sea came and drew her in, out into the bay and down to the bottom of the ocean where she lay. The fish came and feasted on her flesh until there was nothing left but her bones, swaying back and forth on a bed of seaweed. From that day fishermen avoided that place. They believed it to be haunted. Cursed. They kept away.

Then one day a fisherman, new to that part of the coast, came to find work, build himself a home and maybe find himself a wife. He rowed out to that haunted bay, hooked on his bait and cast out his line. He waited all day but no fish took his bait, until, as the sun went down, the line suddenly tightened. His rod bent under the weight of his catch.

What kind of fish was it? Something heavy? He imagined the locals at the market when he carried in the fish to sell. Maybe he'd find a wife there.

He was so busy in his imagination he didn't notice as the skeleton rose out of the water as if dancing on the surface, caught in his line. Then he looked up and saw her.

Terrified, he turned, grabbed the oars and began to row away to the shore, away from the skeleton. Every now and then he looked over his shoulder and saw she was still there dancing on the water behind him. 'It's following me!' he thought.

At the shore he grabbed his rod, jumped onto the beach and ran up the beach towards his tent up on the hill above the beach.

Every now and then he looked over his shoulder and saw the skeleton twisting and bouncing against the rocks, all the time following him.

He reached the door of his tent, threw it open, jumped inside and closed the door behind him. He sat there in the dark and waited and listened.

He sat in the darkness, his heart beating like a drum, but nothing happened. Reassured he got up and lit a candle. As the light filled the tent he saw her, a tangled mess of bones on the floor by the door, blocking his escape.

He saw the clutter of bones and staggered backwards until his back was against the wall, frozen with fright. He waited but nothing happened.

Then he saw the line tangled in the bones. He stood and walked over to them and started to rearrange them, untangling the line and snapping each bone back in its right place until her skeleton was complete and whole.

Then he slipped into bed, pulled his sealskin blanket over his body and fell asleep. As he slept he dreamed – who knows of what? And as he did so a tear ran down his face. As the tear appeared Skeleton Woman moved her head, turning to watch the tear.

Slowly, carefully, she stood and walked over to the bed, bent down and touched the tear with her bony lip. Then she started to sway over him, singing her song. She sang for her flesh to return, for legs so that she could dance, arms to cook, hair so that she might be beautiful once more, lips so that she could speak and kiss – a belly so that she might give birth. In this way, she sang and sang herself back onto her bones. And when she was done, she lay down next to the fisherman and slept.

In the morning, when they awoke, he took her for his wife.

36. The Boy Who Learned to Shudder

This is a ghost story and a comedy, following the narrative collected by the brothers Grimm. Create suspense when you tell it, and pay attention to the descriptions of the various ghouls and monsters. Evoke the character of the son: fearless and matter-of-fact about all his experiences.

A father had two sons. The oldest one was clever and intelligent, and knew how to manage everything, but the youngest one was foolish and could neither understand nor learn anything. When people saw him, they said, 'He will be a burden on his father!' Now when something had to be done, it was always the oldest son who had to do it. However, if the father asked the eldest to fetch anything when it was late, or even worse, at night, and if the way led through the churchyard or some other spooky place, he would always answer, 'Oh, no, father, I won't go there. It makes me shudder!'

The younger son was quite different. He was never afraid. When scary stories were told round the fire at night, he felt no fear at all. Others said, 'That makes me shudder,' but the younger son was puzzled. What could they mean?

One day his father said to him, 'Listen, you there in the corner. You are getting big and strong. You too will have to learn something by which you can earn your living.'

'Well, father,' he answered, 'I do want to learn something. Indeed, if possible I would like to learn how to shudder. I don't understand that at all.'

The oldest son laughed when he heard that, and thought to himself, 'Dear God, what a dimwit that brother of mine is. Nothing will come of him as long as he lives. As the twig is bent, so grows the tree.'

The father sighed, and answered him, 'You may well learn to shudder, but you will not earn your bread by shuddering.'

So the boy went out into the wide world to learn how to shudder with fear.

After some time he arrived at an inn.
'Where are you going?' said the innkeeper.
'I want to learn fear,' he said. 'I want to be able to shudder!'

Hearing this, the innkeeper laughed and said, 'If that's what you want, you've come to the right place.'

'Oh, be quiet,' said the innkeeper's wife. 'Too many people have already lost their lives. It would be a pity and a shame if his beautiful eyes would never again see the light of day.' But the boy said, 'I want to learn to shudder, however difficult it may be. That is why I left home.'

The innkeeper explained that there was a haunted castle not far away where a person could very easily learn how to shudder, if he would just keep watch there for three nights. The king had promised that whoever would dare to do this could have his daughter in marriage, and she was the most beautiful maiden under the sun. Further, in the castle there were great treasures, guarded by evil spirits. These treasures would then be freed, and would make a poor man rich. Many had entered the castle, but no one had come out again alive.

The next morning the boy went to the king and said, 'If it be allowed, I will keep watch three nights in the haunted castle.'

The king looked at him, and because the boy pleased him, he said, 'You may ask for three things to take into the castle with you, but they must be things that are not alive.'

To this the boy replied, 'Then I ask for a fire, a lathe, and a woodcarver's bench with a knife.'

The king had all these things carried into the castle for him during the day. When night was approaching, the boy went inside and made himself a bright fire in one of the rooms, placed the woodcarver's bench and knife beside it, and sat down at the lathe.

'Oh, if only I could shudder!' he said. 'But I doubt if I'll learn it here either.'

Towards midnight he decided to stir up his fire. He was just blowing into it when a cry suddenly came from a corner of the room, 'Au, meow! How cold we are!'
'You fools!' he shouted. 'What are you crying about? If you are cold, come and sit down by the fire and warm yourselves.'

When he had said that, two large black cats came and sat down on either side of him, looking at him savagely with their fiery eyes.

A little while later, after warming themselves, they said, 'Comrade, shall we play a game of cards?'
'Why not?' he replied. 'But first show me your paws.' So they stretched out their claws.
'Oh,' he said, 'what long nails you have. Wait. First I will have to trim them for you.'

With that he seized them by their necks, put them on the woodcarver's bench, and tightened them into the vice by their feet. 'I have been looking at your fingers,' he said, 'and my desire to play cards has disappeared,' and he struck them dead and threw them out through the window into the pond.

He was about to sit down again by his fire, when from every side and every corner there came black cats and black dogs connected by red-hot chains. More and more of them appeared until he could no longer move. They shouted horribly, then jumped into his fire and pulled it apart, trying to put it out.

He quietly watched them for a little while, but finally it was too much for him, and he seized his carving-knife, and cried, 'Away with you, you villains!' and hacked away at them. Some of them ran away, the others he killed and threw out into the pond. When he came back he blew into the embers of his fire until they flamed up again, and warmed himself.

As he sat there, his eyes would no longer stay open, and he wanted to fall asleep. Looking around, he saw a large bed in the corner. 'That is just what I wanted,' he said, and lay down in it. However, as he was about to shut his eyes, the bed began to move by itself, going throughout the whole castle.

'Good,' he said, 'but let's go faster.'

Then the bed rolled on as if six horses were harnessed to it, over thresholds and stairways, up and down. But then suddenly, hop, hop, it tipped upside down and lay on him like a mountain. But he threw the covers and pillows into the air, climbed out, and said, 'Now anyone who wants to may drive.' Then he lay down by his fire, and slept until it was day.

In the morning the king came, and when he saw him lying there on the ground, he thought that the ghosts had killed him and that he was dead. Then said he, 'It is indeed a pity to lose such a handsome person.'

The boy heard this, got up, and said, 'It hasn't come to that yet.' The king was astonished, but glad, and asked how he had fared.

'Very well,' he replied. 'One night is past. The two others will pass as well.'

When he returned to the innkeeper, the latter looked astonished and said, 'I did not think that I'd see you alive again. Did you learn how to shudder?'
'No,' he said, 'it is all in vain. If someone could only tell me how.'

The second night he again went up to the old castle, sat down by the fire, and began his old song once more, 'If only I could shudder!'

As midnight was approaching he heard a noise and commotion. At first it was soft, but then louder and louder. Then it was a little quiet, and finally, with a loud scream, half of a man came down the chimney and fell in front of him.

'Hey!' he shouted. 'Another half belongs here. This is too little.'

Then the noise began again. With roaring and howling the other half fell down as well.

'Wait,' he said. 'Let me blow on the fire and make it burn a little warmer for you.'

When he had done that he looked around again. The two pieces had come together, and a hideous man was sitting in his place.

'That wasn't part of the wager,' said the boy. 'That bench is mine.'

The man wanted to force him aside, but the boy would not let him, instead pushing him away with force, and then sitting down again in his own place. Then still more men fell down, one after the other. They brought nine bones from dead men and two skulls, then set them up and bowled with them.

The boy wanted to play too and said, 'Listen, can I bowl with you?'

'Yes, if you have money.'

'Money enough,' he answered, 'but your bowling balls are not quite round.' Then he took the skulls, put them in the lathe and turned them round.

'There, now they will roll better,' he said. 'Hey! This will be fun!'

He played with them and lost some of his money, but when the clock struck twelve, everything disappeared before his eyes. He lay down and peacefully fell asleep.

The next morning the king came to learn what had happened. 'How did you do this time?' he asked.

'I went bowling,' he answered, 'and lost a few pennies.'

'Did you shudder?'

'How?' he said. 'I had great fun, but if I only knew how to shudder.'

On the third night he sat down again on his bench and said quite sadly, 'If only I could shudder!'

When it was late, six large men came in carrying a coffin. At this he said, 'Aha, for certain that is my little cousin, who died a few days ago.' Then he motioned with his finger and cried out, 'Come, little cousin, come.'

They put the coffin on the ground. He went up to it and took the lid off. A dead man lay inside. He felt his face, and it was cold as ice.

'Wait,' he said, 'I will warm you up a little.' He went to the fire and warmed his own hand, then laid it on the dead man's face, but the dead man remained cold. Then he took him out, sat down by the fire, and laid him on his lap, rubbing the dead man's arms to get the blood circulating again.

When that did not help either, he thought to himself, 'When two people lie in bed together, they keep each other warm.' So he carried the dead man to the bed, put him under the covers, and lay down next to him. A little while later the dead man became warm too and began to move.

The boy said, 'See, little cousin, I got you warm, didn't I?' But the dead man cried out, 'I am going to strangle you.'

'What?' he said. 'Is that my thanks? Get back into your coffin!' Then he picked him up, threw him inside, and shut the lid. Then the six men came and carried him away again.

'I cannot shudder,' he said. 'I won't learn it here as long as I live.'

Then a man came in. He was larger than all others, and looked frightful. But he was old and had a long white beard.

'You wretch,' he shouted, 'you shall soon learn what it is to shudder, for you are about to die.'
'Not so fast,' answered the boy. 'If I am to die, I will have to be where?'
'I've got you,' said the old man.
'Now, now, don't boast. I am just as strong as you are, and probably even stronger.'
'We shall see,' said the old man. 'If you are stronger than I am, I shall let you go. Come, let's put it to the test.'

Then the old man led him through dark passageways to a blacksmith's forge, took an axe, and with one blow drove one of the anvils into the ground.

'I can do better than that,' said the boy, and went to the other anvil. The old man stood nearby, wanting to look on. His white beard hung down. The boy seized the axe and split the anvil with one blow, wedging the old man's beard in the crack.

'Now I have you,' said the boy. 'Now it is your turn to die.' Then he seized an iron bar and beat the old man until he moaned and begged him to stop, promising that he would give him great riches. The boy pulled out the axe and released him.

The old man led him back into the castle, and showed him three chests full of gold in a cellar.

'Of these,' he said, 'one is for the poor, the second one is for the king, and the third one is yours.'

Meanwhile it struck twelve, and the spirit disappeared, leaving the boy standing in the dark.

'I can find my own way out,' he said. Feeling around, he found his way to the bedroom, and fell asleep by his fire.

The next morning the king came and said, 'By now you must have learned how to shudder.'
'No,' he answered. 'What is it? My dead cousin was here, and a bearded man came and showed me a large amount of money down below, but no one showed me how to shudder.' Then the king said, 'You have redeemed the castle, and shall marry my daughter.'
'That is all very well,' said the boy, 'but I still do not know how to shudder.'

Then the gold was brought up, and the wedding celebrated, but however much the young king loved his wife, and however happy he was, he still was always saying, 'If only I could shudder.'

Then, one morning he imagined what would happen if his wife left him. He started to shake and cry. 'I have learned it,' he cried. 'I have learned fear. Look, I am shaking!'

And that's how he finally learned to shudder.

37. The Woodcutter and the Snake

Here's a Serbian story about thinking for yourself, not just going along with the crowd. The nice thing about it is it seems to be about something else and has a great dramatic ending. On the way there are three dreams, which you can develop with atmosphere and description, and a repeating story about giving bad advice to the king where you and your audience can make sections up. I first heard this from Ben Haggarty, who told it right after the 9/11 bombings. A good story to take with you into secondary school life.

Once there was a king who had a dream. He dreamed he was walking through a dark forest. Foxes jumped out, biting and barking, and he woke in a cold sweat.

In the morning he asked his advisors what the dream meant.

'You are as smart as a fox,' said one.

'We should chop down the forest,' said another.

'We should hunt all the foxes,' said a third.

'No,' said the king, 'none of those answers feel right.'

He announced that anyone who could interpret his dream in a way that seemed right would receive three bags of gold.

A woodcutter sitting by a wall in the wood was thinking about this when a snake popped out.

'I am the snake who knows everything,' it said.

'Then do you know the meaning of the king's dream? Tell me and we can share the gold.'

'OK,' said the snake, who told him the meaning of the king's dream.

The woodcutter went off to the king and said, 'The dream means that now is a time of trickery. Be on your guard.'

The king felt that was right and gave him the gold.

The woodcutter went home and kept it all.

A year passed and the king had another dream. He was in the same wood. This time arrows were being fired. He was wounded in the leg and shoulder when he woke up shaking.

In the morning the advisers gave their interpretations:

'You are as sharp as an arrow.'

'We need to train more archers.'

'Kill all the outlaws in the woods.'

'No,' said the king, 'not right.' This time he offered five bags of gold to anyone who could tell him its meaning.

The woodcutter saw an opportunity and returned to the snake burrow and knocked on the wall.

'What do you want?' said the snake who knows everything.

'Sorry about the gold. But would you tell me the meaning of this dream. We'll share the five bags and also I'll pay you what I owe you.'

The snake agreed and explained the dream.

Later at the palace the woodcutter said, 'It means that this will be a time of killing. Your life is in danger and many will die. Be on your guard.'

'That feels right,' said the king and handed over the gold.

The woodcutter went back to the burrow and knocked on the wall. Out came the snake. 'I've got something for you,' said the woodcutter and he whipped out a knife and tried to stab the snake, but it slipped back into the hole faster than the woodcutter could stab.

A year passed and the king had a third dream. He was in the wood looking at a light at the end of the path. He walked out into a green field full of butterflies and sheep, lay down and looked up at the blue sky with a smile on his face.

In the morning he asked the advisers the meaning:
'We need more sheep.'
'You will lead our nation to happiness.'
'The weather will be fine.'
'No,' said the king, 'that's not it!'

He offered seven bags of gold for a good interpretation and the woodcutter saw another opportunity. He went to the burrow and knocked on the wall.
'Sorry,' he said when the snake appeared. 'I was wrong to try and kill you, but now I am truly sorry. Forgive me. If you tell me the meaning of the last dream I'll pay you everything I owe you.' (*That's 1.5 plus 2.5 plus 3.5 = 7.5 bags.*)

The snake agreed and told him.

At the palace he said, 'Your dream means that we are in a time of harmony and happiness. No more danger. Now you can relax and enjoy good times.'
The king was pleased and handed over the gold.

The woodcutter went back to the snake's burrow and knocked.
'Here's the gold,' he said. 'Is that OK? Does that make everything right?'

The snake slithered out of the hole and stood up on tail tip, towering above the man like some great dragon. He hissed and snarled, 'Do you think I care about that!' he said. 'I am the snake who knows everything. I can have anything I want! You are pathetic! You are like some parrot that only copies and never thinks for himself. Look! When it was a time of trickery you tried to trick me; when everyone was killing you tried to kill me; when everyone was being peaceful and loving you were peaceful and loving. What about YOU? You're a unique human being but you behave just like everyone else. Think about that!'

The snake went back to his burrow and the woodcutter went back to his home and thought for a long time about what the snake said.

38. Three Questions

*This Russian folktale was made famous in its retelling by Tolstoy himself.
It asks the big questions about life and comes up with a clear-cut answer to
ponder. It is used by various spiritual teachers as a 'perfect parable'. It's a great
story to take with you on your journey through life. The telling is quite
straightforward, but make sure the sequence of actions by the enemy of the king is
clear, so that we understand how the king saved his own life.*

It once occurred to a certain king, that if he always knew the right time to begin everything; if he knew who were the right people to do things with; and, above all, if he always knew what was the most important thing to do, he would guarantee success in all his works.

So he declared that he would give a great reward to anyone who would teach him those three things: what was the right time for every action, the most important people to deal with, and how he might know what was the most important thing to do.

Learned men came to the king and offered their answers. In reply to the question of right timing, some said that to know the right time for every action, one must draw up in advance a table of days, months and years, and must live strictly according to it. Only in this way could everything be done at its proper time.

Others declared that it was impossible to decide beforehand the right time for every action but that one should always attend to all that was going on, and then do what was most needful.

Others, again, said that however attentive the king might be to what was going on, it was impossible for one man to decide correctly the right time for every action, but that he should have a council of wise men, who would help him to fix the proper time for everything.

But then others said there were some things which could not wait to be laid before a council, but about which one had at once to decide whether to undertake them or not. But in order to decide that, one must know beforehand what was going to happen. It is only magicians who know that; and, therefore, in order to know the right time for every action, one must consult magicians.

There were equally varied answers to the second question. Some said, the people the king most needed were his councillors; others, the priests; others, the doctors; while some said the warriors were the most necessary.

To the third question, as to the most important thing to do: some replied that the most important thing in the world was science. Others said it was skill in warfare; and others, again, that it was religious worship.

The king was not satisfied with any of the answers. Indeed, he noticed a certain self-interest in most of the replies. Doctors promoted doctoring. Priests promoted religion. Magicians promoted magic.

He knew of a wise hermit who lived in solitude deep in the forest, and decided to visit him and ask for his advice. It was known that the hermit would only receive commoners, so the king dressed in simple clothes and set off with his bodyguards for the forest. At the forest's edge he left his horse and asked them to wait for him, and continued alone towards the hermit's hut.

When the king approached, the frail old hermit was digging the ground in front of his hut. When he saw the king he gave him a brief smile and then carried on digging.

The king watched the old man digging: he was obviously tired but he kept on going.

After a while the king said: 'I have come to you, to ask you three questions: How can I learn to do the right thing at the right time? Who are the people I most need to do it, and what is the thing that should be done?'

The hermit listened to the king, but said nothing. He just spat on his hand and recommenced digging.
'You are tired,' said the king, 'let me take the spade and help.'
The hermit gave the spade to the king, and sat down on the ground.
When he had dug two rows, the king stopped and repeated his questions, but the hermit again gave no answer, but rose, stretched out his hand for the spade, and said, 'Now rest and let me work a bit.'

But the king did not give him the spade, and continued to dig. One hour passed, and another. The sun began to sink behind the trees, and the king at last stuck the spade into the ground, and said, 'I came to you, wise man, for an answer to my questions. If you can give me none, tell me so, and I will return home.'
'Here comes someone running,' said the hermit, 'let us see who it is.'

The king turned round, and saw a bearded man come running out of the wood. The man held his hands pressed against his stomach. Blood was flowing from a wound in his belly. When he reached the king, he fell fainting on the ground moaning feebly. The king and the hermit unfastened the man's clothing. There was a large wound in his stomach. The king washed it as best he could, and bandaged it with his handkerchief and with a towel the hermit had. But the blood would not stop flowing.

Again and again the king washed and re-bandaged the wound. Finally the bleeding stopped and the man opened his eyes. The king gave him a drink of water, carried him into the hermit's hut and laid him on a bed where he slept till morning. The king fell asleep too, exhausted from his day's exertions.

When the king woke it was morning and the bearded man was staring at him with tears in his eyes.

'Forgive me!' said the bearded man.
'I do not know you, and have nothing to forgive you for,' said the king.
'You do not know me, but I know you. I am your enemy. Once you had my brother executed and confiscated our family lands. I swore revenge. I came here to kill you: I was waiting to ambush you when you left this place but your bodyguards caught me and I was wounded. Still I got away and came here, where you saved my life. So please, forgive me. I am in your debt and will serve you in any way I can.'
The king smiled, 'Let us now be friends,' he said, 'and both forgive the past. I will restore your family lands when I return to the city.'

The king left his new friend to rest and went outside to look for the hermit, who he found, on his knees, sowing seeds in the beds that had been dug the day before. The king approached him, and said, 'For the last time, I pray you to answer my questions, wise man.'
'You have already been answered!' said the hermit with a grin.
'How answered? What do you mean?' asked the king.
'Do you not see?' replied the hermit. 'If you had not pitied my weakness yesterday, and had not dug those beds for me, but had gone your way, that man would have attacked and killed you. So the most important time was when you were digging the beds; and I was the most important man; and to do me good was your most important business. Afterwards when that man ran to us, the most important time was when you were attending to him, for if you had not bound up his wounds

he would have died without having made peace with you. So he was the most important man, and what you did for him was your most important business.

'Remember then: there is only one time that is important – now! It is the most important time because it is the only time when we have any power.

'The most important person is the one right in front of you; and the most important thing is to do him good, because for that purpose alone we are sent into this life!'

The king was filled with joy at the hermit's words. They guided his rule as king till the end of his days.

39. Gawain and the Green Knight

This is one of the classics of medieval British literature, evoking the world of Arthurian chivalry. The beginning is shocking and gory, the middle can be funny and a bit weird, and the ending is puzzling and surprising.

Long ago, in the castle of Camelot, King Arthur was at table with his knights. It was New Year's Eve and all the knights were there sharing stories and swilling their mead. Just then the door swung open and in rode a huge man, almost a giant, riding a huge horse. It was strange to see a rider in the banquet hall, but stranger still was the colour of this man. He was green from head to toe – green hair, green face, green hands, green teeth – everything was green. He had fearsome flaming eyes and carried a huge axe in one hand.

'You are welcome,' said Arthur from his throne. 'Tell me friend, what brings you here? Will you eat with us tonight?'
'NO!' he growled, 'I am not here to eat. I'm here to challenge you. Do any of your knights dare this challenge? Tonight chop into my neck with this axe, and then in a year's time if I am able, I will do the same to whoever tries his luck with me.'

Sir Gawain, Arthur's most perfect knight, quickly stepped forward.
'I will do it!' he said.

The Green Knight dismounted, knelt down in front of Gawain, handed him the axe, and bent down so Gawain could swing the axe at his neck. Gawain lifted the heavy axe up in to the air, let it swing down and... whhhhsh... it sliced clean through the green man's neck. His head rolled down over the floor and under the table. Gawain was just about to raise his hand in a salute of victory when he noticed that the Green Knight's body was still kneeling and headless. As he watched, the body stood, walked over to the table, reached underneath it and took hold of its own head by the hair. Then the head spoke, 'See you in a year, Gawain. Ask for the Green Lodge. You can meet me there.'

Winter turned to spring, spring to summer and summer to autumn and when the first snows of winter began to fall Gawain set off in search of the Green Lodge. Everywhere he asked about the Green Lodge, but nobody knew where to find it.

Then on Christmas Eve he was riding down a valley when he saw a large manor house on the road. He rode up the drive and was greeted by a huge man with a big bushy beard and bright staring eyes.

'I am the Baron,' he said. 'This is my home. What brings you here?'
'I seek the Green Lodge,' he said.
'You are near your journey's end. It is one hour's ride from here. Stay for a few days, rest and then be on your way.'
Gawain was tired and happily agreed.
That evening Gawain sat at the table between the Baron and his beautiful young wife. All evening she talked with him, smiling and laughing as they talked.

Before bed the Baron said, 'Tomorrow I will go hunting. You stay here and rest. Whatever I catch I will give to you. Whatever you win while I am away you must give to me. Do you agree?'
Gawain nodded.

The next morning Gawain was resting in bed when there was a knock on the door and the young wife slipped in and sat on the edge of his bed.

'Hello,' she said, smiling.

'What are you doing here?' said Gawain. 'You shouldn't come into my bedroom!'

'Oh, I just want a kiss!' she said giggling, leant over and kissed him on the cheek, then left.

That evening the Baron came back from hunting and Gawain was there to welcome him. He threw a brace of rabbits at Gawain's feet.

'That's what I won. What did you get?'

Gawain walked over to the Baron and kissed him on the cheek!

'I see,' said the Baron. 'Then let's do the same thing tomorrow. I'll hunt and you rest. Whatever each of us wins in the day we will give to the other.'

The next morning the Baron's wife came into his bedroom again and sat on the bed.

'Out!' shouted Gawain.

'In a minute,' she said, leaned down and kissed Gawain on both cheeks.

'Bye!' and she giggled her way out of the room.

That evening the Baron came back with a wild boar.

'This is for you,' he said to Gawain. 'What have you got for me?' Gawain walked over to the Baron and kissed both of his cheeks.

'Good man!' said the Baron. 'Same again tomorrow?'

'Fine!' said Gawain.

The next morning, with the Baron off hunting, she came into his room again. This time she took off a green garter from her leg and gave it to him.

'Keep this for me!' she said and kissed him straight on the lips!

That evening when the Baron came back he gave Gawain a wild deer. In return

Gawain went up to the Baron and kissed him on the lips. But he didn't give him the garter...

The next day, following the Baron's directions, Gawain arrived at the Green Lodge, and saw the Green Knight outside sharpening his axe.
'Good,' said the Knight. 'Just in time. Come over here!'
Gawain dismounted and knelt down ready to face death. The Green Knight stood above him, swung back the axe and then swung it down at Gawain's neck... but stopped the swing just before it touched him.
'That's for the first day, when you kissed me once!' he said, laughing.

Gawain was puzzled and glanced up at the Knight. He looked familiar but... The axe swung down again, and again stopped just short of his neck.

'That was for the second day, when you kissed me twice.' Gawain looked again. The Green Knight looked just like the Baron. Could it be the same person? The axe swung a third time and this time just nicked Gawain's neck so that three drops of blood fell onto his tunic.
'And that's for the third time. You kept your word with the kiss but kept the garter for yourself. That cut is for the garter.'

Gawain was confused. 'So... you are the Baron?'
'Yes,' he said. 'You passed the test of honesty well enough. Now you can go home. Happy New Year!'

So Gawain, relieved, went home and told the story to the Knights of the Round Table.

At the end of the story he said, '...and I feel so bad. I kept the garter and broke my word. I have failed you all.'
'Not at all,' said Arthur. 'On the contrary, we all honour you and your courage. You

have been brave and honest and also you have been human. Nobody is perfect, not even you, Gawain, and that's just fine. From now on let us all wear a green garter to remind us all that nobody is perfect, not even a Knight of the Round Table. In the end we are all imperfect and human.'

Everyone cheered, the music played and the mead flowed and they danced and danced and danced.

40. Mother Sun and Her Daughters

This story, from Argentina, evokes cycles of having children and leaving home. It provides a mythical and magical take on the subject. I love the way it cycles and that in this story the mother is the sun. Anyone who has ever had or been a parent can connect with this story.

Once, Mother Sun would dance across the sky every day surrounded by her twelve daughters. She loved them and they loved her and she shined with happiness.

As they danced across the sky they sang an ancient song.

> *Dawn to dusk, dusk to dawn*
> *The sun will shine, the moon will dance*
> *Dusk to dawn, dawn to dusk*
> *We feel the mountains call*

In the evenings the daughters would look down over the edge of the sky down to earth. They saw fires, they saw men, and they saw dancing, heard singing.

They said, 'Mama, can we go down there?'

'Why would you want that?' she said, nervously. 'Everything is perfect up here.'

Then one night, under their mother's bed, they found a rope made from their mother's dreams. They hooked it to the edge of the sky and climbed down to the earth, singing their song.

The men stopped dancing and watched as the girls slipped down the rope, singing:

> *Dawn to dusk, dusk to dawn*
> *The sun will shine, the moon will dance*
> *Dusk to dawn, dawn to dusk*
> *We feel the mountains call*

They led them over to the fire. The drummers drummed, the players played and the daughters danced and danced with their new friends.

Raven was watching.

'Time for a change!' he croaked to himself.

He flew to the rope of dreams.

He flew up to the place it met the sky.

He cut through the rope with his sharp beak and it fell to the ground.

At dawn the daughters looked for the rope to climb back to their mother but it was gone, so they returned to the fires and stayed with their men. Soon they were all married. In a way they were happy to be married but there was also a feeling of having been tricked into it – an unspoken resentment towards their husbands.

Now Mother Sun was sad. She gazed down at her daughters and cried. Her light was weak and her journey across the sky was swift. It was winter. She missed them so much. There was no more singing and dancing. Only grieving.

Then one evening she looked over the edge of the sky into a cave, down into the eyes of Jaguar Man. She wove a rope of her dreams, hooked it to the edge of the sky and climbed down into his cave.

Now she was happier.

She visited him every night.

Then one day she felt her belly swelling. She no longer visited Jaguar Man.

She waited as her belly grew round and huge.

She gave birth to twelve new daughters and hid that rope of dreams under her bed. Soon they all danced and shone across the sky, singing and smiling.

> *Dawn to dusk, dusk to dawn*
> *The sun will shine, the moon will dance*
> *Dusk to dawn, dawn to dusk*
> *We feel the mountains call*

Time passed and in the evenings the daughters peered down towards earth...

41. Five Wise Trainings

Here's an Indian story about finding rules and principles from which to live your life. It has all sorts of plot variety within it. Pay attention to the ending: make sure it is clear how and why the king's brother was killed.

Once there was a boy called Ram Sing, who lived in a little village on the edge of a wide shimmering desert. His family was very poor and often they went to bed hungry.

One day his father told him he should leave home, leave school and travel to the city to find work as there was not enough food to go round. Ram Sing agreed. He packed a small sack with food and a few clothes and went off to the temple to speak to the wise old monk who lived there. The old man had been a friend to Ram Sing since he was a baby. Ram was going to miss him.

'I have to leave now,' said Ram Sing. 'Tell me how I should behave in the wide world. What is it like? I have never left this village!'

The old man smiled, 'You are a good young man,' he said. 'Behave in the world as you do in this village, with kindness and courtesy, and you will do well. Here are five rules – try and keep them and they will protect you from harm.
'First, work hard: this will lead to success. Second, be kind: this will lead to safety. Third, be truthful: this will lead to trust.
'Fourth, be humble: this will lead to friendship.

'Fifth, listen to those wiser than you: this will lead to wisdom.'

Ram Sing bowed, left the temple and started off across the desert. As he walked he replayed the conversation over and over in his mind, trying hard to remember the five things he should do.

After three days and nights he came to a city and, hungry and tired, he went to the marketplace. He looked around, saw a man dressed in fine expensive robes, and went up to him.

'Excuse me, sir,' he said, 'I am new in this town and need a job. I am young and strong and will do whatever work is needed. Can you help me?'

The man looked Ram up and down and smiled.

'As it happens the chief minister needs a personal servant. You look honest and trustworthy. Would you like the job?'

Ram Sing nodded and smiled and within the hour he was working for the minister.

A few weeks later the minister and the king were travelling across the desert with a caravan of servants and soldiers, on the way to the neighbouring kingdom. Halfway across they ran out of water. They stopped at the next village and asked for water but the villagers said they had none to spare, there was just a little for themselves.

The king was not pleased and shouted at the minister to find water. The minister bowed and told Ram Sing to solve the problem. Ram Sing remembered the monk's advice to work hard. He bowed to the minister. 'I will do my best,' he said.

He walked off into the village asking everyone he saw if there was a way to find water. At first everyone just shook their heads but finally a very old little man said, 'There is an old well on the edge of town, but we don't use it. Everyone who goes there never comes back!'

Ram Sing took two buckets and set off for the well. When he got there he saw a staircase leading deep down into the ground. He went deeper and deeper into the ground until it was completely dark. Finally his toes touched water and he started to fill the buckets. Just then he saw a light coming down the staircase. As it came closer he saw a huge giant carrying a flaming torch in one hand and clutching a pile of bones to his chest with the other. The giant looked angry. Ram Sing kept quiet.

The giant stared down at him, growled and looked at the bones.
'What do you think of my wife then?' he said.
Ram thought about it. The bones must have been his wife. He must have loved her. What should he say? Maybe he thinks she's still alive!
Just then he remembered the monk's second piece of advice: to be kind. But also he should speak the truth. What should he say?
'I am sure,' he said, 'there is no other like her in all the world.' The giant smiled.
'You answer well,' he said. 'Others have said she is just a pile of bones and I have killed them for that. But you were kind. How can I reward you?'
'Well,' said Ram. 'I'd like you to stop haunting this well please and let people drink from it again.'
'OK!' said the giant, and disappeared.

An hour later Ram returned to the king with buckets brimming with sweet cold water and told them where to get more. He then went and told the villagers that the well was safe and they were delighted.

The king was impressed too. 'Now you can work for me!' he said.

Back in the city, Ram Sing worked as a clerk in the king's office, working hard and always trying to speak the truth. Soon he became trusted by all and rose through the ranks till he was the chief treasurer.

This made the king's brother jealous. The brother liked to steal money from the king's treasury but with Ram Sing in charge it was difficult. One day he came to Ram and said,

'My friend. You are now one of the most important persons in the kingdom. We should be friends. Let me offer you my daughter as your bride and then you will be like a royal family member. Better than ordinary people. Marry her!'

Ram Sing was tempted, but it didn't feel right. He remembered the words of the old monk (be humble) and politely declined.

This made the brother angry and he decided to plot against him. He went to the king and said, 'Brother, that Ram Sing is speaking against you. He says he would make a better king than you. He wants to be king. You must do something!'

The king believed his brother and hatched a plan.

There was a building project by the western gate that Ram had been supervising. The king sent two guards there saying, 'When someone comes and asks when the project will be finished, chop off his head and bring it to me in a bag.'

The guards went off and Ram Sing was summoned. 'Go to the building project by the western gate,' the king said, 'and ask them when it will be finished.'

Ram set off toward the gate but on the way he heard the sound of teaching coming from a temple. Remembering the monk's advice about listening to those wiser than oneself, he went into the temple to listen to the talk. He became so absorbed in the teaching he lost all sense of time.

Meanwhile the king's brother was impatient. He went to the king and asked what had happened.

'I have sent Ram Sing to the western gate where he will be killed. I am just waiting for his head to be delivered.'

They waited for a while and then the brother left and rode out to the gate. He stopped at the building project and asked the guards, 'Well! Has it been done? When will it be done?'

The guard swung his sword and the brother's head rolled. They put it in a sack and set off back for the palace.

Meanwhile, the king had lost patience and was riding out to the gate to see what had happened. As he passed by the temple Ram Sing heard the clatter of hooves, turned and saw the king and ran out to him.

At the same moment the guards met the king in the street.
'We have done as you asked,' said the guards and handed the king the bag.
The king looked at Ram Sing, puzzled. Then he looked in the bag and was shocked.

He kept quiet and made an investigation, which revealed his brother's treachery. Ram Sing remained treasurer and lived long and happily in the king's palace.

When he had children of his own he taught them the five trainings to protect you in life: Work hard, be kind, be truthful, be humble, and listen to the wise.

With such good advice they did well when it was their turn to go out into the wide world, avoiding harm and finding happiness.

42. Gawain Gets Married

Here's another Arthurian tale about Gawain. This one provides a chance to look at differences between men and women, and gives a tip or two for successful relationships. Milk the ugliness of the old crone for maximum impact. Get lots of audience suggestions about what Arthur found on his research trip.

One summer's evening at the court of King Arthur, the knights were feasting and drinking and telling their stories when the door of the hall was flung open and in ran a woman. Her clothes were those of a noble woman, but were torn and dirty. She had a tear- streaked face and cuts on her arms and feet.

She ran to the throne of the king and knelt before him. 'Your majesty, I come to you for justice. The Black Knight came to my castle and burned it to the ground. He killed my husband and my three children and took others away as slaves. He is evil and must be stopped. Please, will you help me?'

Arthur nodded. 'I have heard of this Black Knight. Tomorrow I will ride to his castle and challenge him.'

The next day Arthur rode off through the English wildwood to the Black Knight's castle. When he arrived he stopped. It was a huge dark building surrounded by a wide moat with the smell of death. No way in. He rode around the castle three times. On the third circle a drawbridge appeared where there had been none before and he rode inside.

The courtyard was empty and silent as death. Arthur dismounted and was about to shout out his challenge, when he found himself frozen to the spot. He couldn't move anything from the neck down. Some enchantment was working on him so he just stood there and waited.

A while later a knight appeared wearing black armour over the whole of the body and a black helmet with a visor down over the face. No skin showed anywhere. The knight walked over to Arthur, drew a sword and pressed it against Arthur's neck.

'Welcome, Arthur,' hissed a voice from behind the visor. 'Now you are here, I think I will kill you.'

'I challenge you to a duel,' said Arthur. 'A fair duel. Will you fight?'

'Why should I bother with that stuff?' hissed the voice. 'I can just kill you now... no, maybe I'll set you a challenge. You can either accept the challenge or I'll kill you now. What's it going to be?'

'Ummm... I'll take the challenge.'

'Good, so here's your task. Find the answer to this question: what is it that the women of the world really want? You have a year to get the right answer. Come back here in a year's time and if you don't get it right then I'll chop off your head. Do you agree?'

'OK,' said Arthur.

The knight disappeared and moments later Arthur found he could move his body. He rode out of the castle and off to find the answer. Arthur travelled from place to place, asking everyone he met what they thought women really wanted. Men said one thing, women said other things, but Arthur was never really sure if he had the right answer.

After a year of travel he was riding back to the Black Knight's castle, preparing to lose his head, when he saw an old lady sitting by a bush. She was the ugliest lady he had ever seen. Matted hair, corkscrew nose and twisted chin. Her teeth were black and her skin had a greenish hue. 'Hello,' she said.

'Hello,' said Arthur.

'I know the answer to your riddle,' she said.

'Really?' said Arthur.

'Yes,' she said, 'but if I tell you I need something from you. Find me a young handsome knight to marry me. Do that and I'll tell you the answer.'

'OK,' said Arthur, 'I'll do my best.'

She told him the answer to the riddle.

Back in the castle Arthur returned to the courtyard and again found himself frozen to the spot. Out came the Black Knight, covered from head to toe in black armour.

'Well,' said the knight. 'What do women really want?'

'Handbags?' said Arthur.

'No!'

'Husbands?'

'NO!'

'Diamonds?'

'NO!'

This went on for a while, then the knight said, 'If you can't do better than that, Arthur, you don't deserve to live.'

'OK,' Arthur said, 'then I'll tell you. This is the true answer. Women want sovereignty: to be able to choose their own path. Just as a king rules over his kingdom, so women want to be able to rule over themselves.'

The knight hissed, 'How did you know that? How could you get that right?'

'Who are you?' said Arthur.

The knight took off the helmet and Arthur gasped. Long hair as black as a raven's back flowed out. Fair white skin and blood red lips. It was his half-sister, Morgana.'Why?' he said. 'Why did you do this? Why did you kill that poor woman's family?'

'Oh, you silly man!' she said. 'That was all just a story. I made it up to get you here. You are so busy with dragons and rescuing maidens I thought you needed some education. That's all. Now you can go.'

She disappeared and Arthur returned to his castle, where he told the story to his knights. When he had finished his story he said, 'So now I need a volunteer, to keep my promise.' The room went quiet. Knights were looking at the floor.
'I need a husband for the old woman. Who will marry her?'
He waited for a while and then young, handsome Gawain stood up.
'I will do it, your majesty. I will marry her, for you.'
The other knights clapped and breathed a sigh of relief. 'He's really brave!' they thought.

The next day Gawain rode to the bush where he found the old lady.
'Hello,' she said, grinning through her few blackened teeth. 'You must be my husband. Will you marry me?'
Gawain stared at her wrinkled twisted old face and her gummy mouth. Then he took a deep breath.
'I will,' he said.
'Oh goodie! Let's go back to the castle.'
She jumped up behind him on the horse and they rode back to Camelot.

They were married the same day. There was a small feast, but Gawain was not feeling very cheerful. Every time he looked at the old lady his heart sank.
'All my life I dreamed I would marry a perfect, beautiful woman, and instead I marry an old hag!'

After the feast they went to their bedroom. The old lady slipped under the covers and waited for Gawain to join her. He came a while later and lay in the bed, right on the edge, as far away from the old lady as possible.

'What's the matter, husband?' she cried. 'Don't you like me?'

He turned towards her and caught a blast of her foul, rotting breath.

'Kiss me!' she said, giggling.

With his mind firmly on duty Gawain closed his eyes, leaned over and kissed the old lady firmly on the lips. It was odd. They seemed strangely soft. He opened his eyes and in front of him was a lovely young woman with clear skin, ruby lips and long silky hair.

'Who are you?' he said.

'I am your wife,' she said. 'I was cursed to have the form of an old woman till I found a husband who could accept me the way I am. With your kiss you broke the spell.'

'Wow!' said Gawain. 'That's great news!'

'Yes,' she said. 'Now I can be young like this half the time and old the other half. It's up to you, husband. Would you like me young in the day and old at night, or the other way round?'

Gawain thought about it. He remembered Arthur's story about what women want. 'What would you like?' he asked. She shrieked with delight.

'Oh Gawain, now you have broken the other half of the spell. I was to stay half and half, old and young, till I found a husband who wanted what was best for me. Now there is no spell and I can be cute like this all the time. Hooray. You are my hero!'

They delighted in each other's company and in the morning they went down to breakfast to the admiration of the court. When Gawain told his story the knights clapped.

'You deserve her,' they said. 'You are the bravest of knights.'

And so they lived as husband and wife happily until the end of their days.

43. Everything You Need

Here's a powerful and somewhat gruesome story from Iraq. It's full of tension and descriptive power – not for the faint-hearted, but certainly memorable and replete with learnings. The main thing is to evoke the character of Abdul and his desperation, and then the shock and horror of the various catastrophes. You can find more like this in a wonderful collection called Tales from the Arab Tribes *by C.G. Campbell, who collected the stories in southern Iraq about 100 years ago.*

Once in the ancient city of Basra there was a poor carpenter, Abdul, who lived with his wife in a tumbled down shack on the edge of town. When it rained the rain poured through holes in the roof, soaking husband and wife alike as they shivered in the cold.

On one such day a damp Abdul was sitting in an inn sipping coffee when he overheard a stranger talking at the next table. He was eating fine food and sipping sweet drinks. Abdul watched with jealousy and felt his empty tummy rumble.

He listened to the stranger talking about his life in the desert and how there was buried wealth there.

'Under the desert I know of a tunnel that will lead a man to great wealth. Few dare enter the tunnel. There is talk of the ghosts and spirits that guard it but I say that is just old superstition. Anyone who has the courage to travel this tunnel will find more gold than they can ever count. Those who had the courage to travel to those treasure houses will find great wealth. Those who are frightened of superstitions and ghosts will remain poor. Do any of you have such courage? If so I can promise you more gold than you can hold in your hands, more jewels than you can count on your fingers, and more knowledge than you can ever speak of. Do any of you have the courage?'

The group around the table murmured the name of God and said that no, they would not go near the spirits of the desert, but Abdul, damp and cold, called out: 'I will do it! I have no such fear. Take me to the tunnel!'

The man smiled and nodded. The next day they took two camels out into the desert and travelled deep into the golden sand. They stopped by a ruined stone hut and stepped inside the walls. The man got down on his knees and started digging in the sand with his hands, revealing a brass door underneath.

Written on the door were the words:

> *He who enters here will have more gold than he can carry, more jewels than he can count and more knowledge than he can speak of. Kiss the door to enter.*

Thinking of his leaky roof and his unhappy wife, Abdul kissed the door. It slid open revealing a stone staircase going deep down under the earth.

'You're on your own from here,' said the man and settled down in the shade of the wall.

Abdul walked down the stairs thinking of all the money he would soon own, the house he would buy and the wonderful things he would fill it with.

The steps went deeper and deeper into the cold clammy depths of the desert. He stopped at a tunnel lit by flaming torches and he walked for what seemed like hours till he came to a second door with the same words on it.

He who enters here will have more gold than he can carry, more jewels than he can count and more knowledge than he can speak of. Kiss the door to enter.

Abdul kissed the door and it swung open and he stepped inside.

At first he saw only darkness, but as his eyes adjusted to the dark he realised he was in a huge cavern. Skeletons hung from the cave walls, staring at him from their boney sockets. In the centre of the cave was a huge pile of gold. Abdul was just about to fill his pockets when a voice boomed down from the top of the golden hoard.
'Come!' she said. 'Kiss me and the treasure you seek will be yours.'
On top of the gold a woman sat with long black hair, covered in golden jewellery.
'Kiss me!' she repeated.

Abdul scrambled up the pile of coins and at the top he leaned over and kissed her.

Immediately he knew something was wrong. He couldn't pull away. Something was pulling on his tongue harder and harder. Blood filled his mouth as his tongue was ripped out of his mouth. Then something else, another tongue, entered his mouth and took its place. Then the woman was gone, dissolving into mist and he was alone with a strange tongue in his mouth.

Abdul was terrified. He tried to pray but the tongue pressed into his throat and choked him till he stopped the prayer.

'You do as I say!' it commanded, speaking through Abdul's own mouth. The tongue ordered Abdul to go back to Basra and, terrified, Abdul obeyed.

He walked alone through the desert till he came to the city and the tongue ordered him to go to an inn where his friends were drinking coffee.
Then the tongue began to speak.
He said to one of his friends 'Do you know that your brother has been stealing

from your shop? Every day he takes money and hides it under his bed. If you don't believe me go and see.'

The brother rushed home, found the gold and soon the two brothers were fighting. Soon one was stabbed in the belly.

To another friend he said, 'Do you know that your wife no longer loves you? Soon she will ask for a divorce.'
The friend believed the tongue and went home in tears.

One by one the tongue whispered poison to Abdul's friends until every face in the inn was black with anger.

Then the tongue ordered Abdul to go home.

Abdul's wife came out to greet him, but as she approached the tongue called out: 'I divorce you, I divorce you, and I divorce you.'
The wife could not believe her ears and ran away in tears.

Then Abdul's only son came out of the house.
'Go to the well!' ordered the tongue, 'and stand on its edge.'

The boy was frightened at the strange sound of his father's voice but he did as he was told and stood on the well's edge. Then the tongue gave a horrible shriek, giving the son such a fright that he slipped and fell down to the bottom of the well.

Abdul ran away into the streets of Basra trying to think of a way to get rid of the tongue, keeping away from anybody in case the tongue should do any more harm.

He left the city and wandered through the desert till he came to a deep wide river. As he approached for a drink he saw a holy man reciting prayers by the river.

The man stared at Abdul and pointed a staff at his mouth. He felt the tongue being pulled away, pulled out of his mouth, out and away. As it left his mouth he saw that it was a thick black snake.

At that moment Abdul fell into the water with blood pouring from his mouth. Four huge shark-like fish swam towards him and began to eat him alive, one feeding on each limb.

By the time the holy man had pulled him from the water his arms and legs were gone. The holy man brought a doctor and cared for Abdul till his wounds had healed. He could not speak or write or tell his story to others, but the holy man arranged a place for him to beg in the market. In this way he lived for many years, fed by the good people of Basra city. Every day other beggars helped him to eat and drink, and when coins were dropped in his begging cup they took them for him as he could not do anything for himself.

In this way Abdul lived until he died. On his grave they left a plaque:

'Here is a man who found more gold that he could hold in his hands, more jewels than he could count on his fingers and more knowledge than he could ever speak of.'

44. Gilgamesh

This is one of the first stories to be written down (on clay tablets) and is one of the most wonderful in the storytelling repertoire. It's a huge, many-layered epic of the king of Uruk, moving through friendship, adventure and finally the facing of mortality as the king learns to be a king. This is a short text with some of its best bits.

Once, in the city of Uruk, King Gilgamesh was out of control. He took what he wanted, whenever he wanted it, from anybody. If he wanted food, he took it. If he wanted a wife, he took her. If he wanted a house, he took it. If anyone stood in his way he crushed them with his brute power. He was the king and he did what he wanted. No one could match him in strength. No one could stand against him.

The people of Uruk prayed to the gods.
'Help us!' they said. 'King Gilgamesh does what he wants. He does nothing for the good of his people. He is out of control!'

The gods and goddesses agreed that Gilgamesh needed a friend, an equal, someone to match his power, so they took a ball of clay and threw it down from the heavens to a wasteland outside Uruk. As it hit the ground it turned into a wild man, Enkido.

Enkido lived there for some time as an animal grazing with a herd of deer, protecting them from danger and breaking up the traps the hunters set for them. One hunter saw Enkido, went to Uruk and reported him to Gilgamesh. 'He is a giant, your majesty. As tall and as wide as you. He lives like an animal, covered only in thick long hair.'

'Send him a wife!' said Gilgamesh. 'She will make him into a man.'

They sent a woman from the temple to civilise the wild man. She waited for him in the wasteland, silent and still. When his herd came grazing he scented her. She called to him and he came, sniffing and snorting, not understanding what she was at all. Soon her scent was in him and the herd ran from the smell, leaving Enkido alone with his new wife.

She took him to the city.
She taught him to eat from a plate.
She taught him to drink from a cup. She taught him to speak.
She taught him all this and more.
Then she took him to the streets of Uruk and waited there.

Gilgamesh was walking to the house of a newly married couple, when Enkido stood in his way. Gilgamesh pushed him but he stood as solid as a tree. Gilgamesh hit him but he would not budge. Then the two giant men clashed, wrestling together for hours with such force that the walls of the city itself shook as they fought. Finally Gilgamesh forced Enkido down on one knee. 'It is over!' he said. The two men embraced and vowed to be friends forever.

From that day Gilgamesh and Enkido were inseparable. They ate together, swam together, wrestled together, played together. Gilgamesh no longer roamed the city taking what he should not. He had a friend.

Then Gilgamesh decided that he needed an adventure.

'Come, my brother. Let us go to the Cedar Forest and kill the monster, Humbaba, who lives there. Let's do that now, so our names will be known forever for such a great deed.'

Enkido was not sure. 'Brother, Humbaba is a terrible and huge creature. Are you sure?'
'I will go. I must go. Are you with me?'

In order to protect him, Enkido went along. They walked to the forest, covering in a day what would take most men a year. They were huge and marvellous. They walked and walked for three days and three nights until they came to the forest, and in the forest they followed the huge footsteps of Humbaba till they came to his den.

He was as tall as the tallest cedar. As vast as a mountain. He opened his cavern-mouth, showed his sword teeth, and roared.
'Prepare to die!' he cried and rushed out towards them.
Gilgamesh and Enkido drew their swords and rushed towards the great monster, roaring like two wild bulls.
The sun god, friend of Gilgamesh, saw their courage and threw a wind down at Humbaba, pinning him to the ground. Humbaba could not move. Gilgamesh put his axe to the monster's throat. In three strokes of the axe he was dead.

Then they chopped down mighty cedars and made a raft, floated it down the river back to Uruk. Gilgamesh carried Humbaba's head as his trophy.

Back in Uruk, one goddess was in love with Gilgamesh. She went to him. 'Be my husband,' she said.
Gilgamesh refused. She felt insulted. She was angry.
Furious, she plotted revenge. She went to the gods and complained about Gilgamesh.

'They have broken the law. They have killed the forest guardian. They must pay. Let us send them the great bull of heaven. He will kill them.'

The great bull attacked the two friends but they killed it easily. But that night Enkido had a dream that the gods were meeting to decide his fate. In his dream the angry goddess spoke to the others: 'They have killed Humbaba, cut down the sacred trees and killed the bull of heaven. One of them must die!'

The gods debated and decided that Enkido must die.

When Enkido woke he said to Gilgamesh, 'I dreamed that I will die. I feel it will be soon.'
'NO!' Gilgamesh roared and strutted but could do nothing. His friend died and Gilgamesh laid his body out on a table, refusing to believe his friend had gone. Then a maggot crawled out of Enkido's nostril.

Gilgamesh tore off his clothes and wearing only a lion skin he marched out of Uruk wild with confusion and grief.
'I will go to the man who has won everlasting life,' he said. 'He will teach me the secret, then I will not be defeated by death. Then perhaps I can save my friend.'

He walked to the tunnel to the other worlds, where the sun races under the earth between dusk to dawn. He waited till sunrise and began to run, running and running to get to the end of the tunnel before sunset when the tunnel would fill with the sun and burn him alive. He ran and ran and made it just in time.

He came to a man on the shore of a lake: a ferryman, surrounded by his stone oarsmen. Gilgamesh ran at them, wild and crazy, and smashed every stone man to pieces. Then he said to the ferryman, 'Take me across the lake to the one who is immortal. Take me!'

'You have smashed my crew!' said the ferryman. 'But cut me one hundred long straight poles from the forest, and I can take you there.'

Gilgamesh rushed at the forest, cutting and cleaning the poles till they were ready, then they boarded the raft. Each pole was used to punt the raft once, and then was dropped into the Sea of Death. To touch that sea means death. In this way they travelled to the opposite shore.

Gilgamesh stepped onto the shore and stared at a thin old man sitting on the beach.
'I seek the one who won immortality,' he said. 'Tell me where to find him.'
'You have found him,' said the man. 'I am he!'
'Then tell me your secret. How may I win immortality?'
'First stay awake for one week, then I will tell you!'
'Fine!' said Gilgamesh. He sat by the shore and immediately fell asleep.
The immortal looked at Gilgamesh and thought, 'When he wakes he will deny that he slept. I shall give him proof.'

Every day his wife baked a loaf of bread and left it in front of Gilgamesh. When he woke after seven days he saw seven loaves, one fresh that day, one covered in mould after the full week, and the others somewhere in between.

'You slept,' said the immortal. 'You have failed. Now go home! But before you go I will tell you this. In the deep ocean there is a green spiny plant. It holds the secret of youth.'

Gilgamesh tied great stones onto his legs and jumped into the great deep. He took the plant in his hand and set off with it back to Uruk. On the way he came to a lake. Leaving the plant by the lake he bathed in the water. While he was bathing a snake came and took the plant away, leaving only a snakeskin behind.

So Gilgamesh returned to Uruk empty-handed, without the secret of eternal life.

Without the herb of eternal youth. Yet somehow now he was ready to rule.
He no longer just took what he wanted, whenever he wanted it.
If he wanted food, he asked for it.
If he wanted a wife, he asked the family.
If he wanted a house, he bought it.
If anyone stood in his way, he reasoned with them.

He ruled wisely, doing his best for Uruk and its people.
He was now a great king.
He remained great till his dying day.

That is the tale of Great King Gilgamesh, whose stories were written on clay tablets – the oldest written story in the human world.

45. A Drop of Honey

This is a great story for talking about conflict and escalation. It is found in the Arabian Nights *collection and has also been collected in Iran, Burma and Thailand. Evoke the indifference of the king and the progressive escalation of violence step by step.*

Once there was a shepherd from the Western Land. Every spring he took his goats across the river and up into the mountains of the Eastern Land, fattening his flock on the rich mountain grass until autumn, when the snows drove him back west to his village. For half the year he lived on milk, cheese and mutton from his flock, his only companion his beloved sheepdog. For the rest of the year he rested in the comfort of his family home. In this way the years passed.

One autumn the old shepherd, with his flock and dog, was making his way, as usual, down a mountain pass in the Eastern Land, when he passed a village with a large wooden sign advertising an inn and store just around the corner. The shepherd felt a longing for something sweet after nothing but milk and meat for so long. He left his goats grazing on the verge and stepped into the store with his beloved collie at his heels. The shopkeeper welcomed him in the Eastern tongue and, speaking a little himself, the shepherd asked whether he might buy a single spoonful of honey, as he had tasted nothing sweet for months. Although a little disappointed by the paltry scale of the transaction, the shopkeeper nodded his agreement politely and walked over to a large wooden barrel in the corner of the shop with a small metal spoon in his hand while the shepherd stood and waited.

Now, the king of the Eastern Land and his chief minister were in the habit of dressing up in disguise and wandering around the country. On that day the king and minister were sitting drinking coffee in the same shop where the shepherd was waiting for his honey.

The king was pleased that the owner had shown such courtesy to this Westerner by agreeing to his request. He watched as the innkeeper walked towards the barrel. He watched as the spoon was dipped into the honey. He watched as the shopkeeper walked carefully back across the room, the spoon brimming with golden amber.

The minister noticed that, as the shopkeeper walked, the honey on the underside of the spoon was collecting together into a single drop which hung tenuously from the centre of the spoon's base, growing larger moment by moment. He whispered playfully to the king.
'Look! In a moment some honey is going to drip onto the floor. Should we tell him?'
'Not our problem!' laughed the king.

They watched as the weight of the honey drop pulled against its attachment to the spoon and followed its fall down onto the stone slab next to the shepherd's worn old boots. Meanwhile the shepherd gratefully accepted the spoon, placed it in his mouth, and with eyes closed he let the sweetness dissolve onto his taste buds, savouring every sweet moment. While this was going on a large green bluebottle flew past the shepherd's legs and, catching the scent of the drop of honey on the stone floor, immediately changed course and began to descend towards the sweet mound.

The keen-eyed minister noticed this.
'Look, your majesty,' he whispered. 'The bluebottle is going for the honey on the floor. Should we do anything?'

'Definitely not our problem!' said the king.

The shopkeeper had a cat who hated bluebottles. She was sitting by the shepherd, warming herself on a sunlit patch of the floor when she saw the bluebottle veering in her direction. In an instant her muscles were tensed and she was ready to pounce. The minster was watching all this, and pointed it out to the king, who just shrugged and watched.

When the insect was within range the cat jumped, claws stretched, teeth bared, soaring through the air and catching it between her teeth, killing it instantly. However, the momentum of the cat continued to carry her horizontally through the air in the direction of the shepherd's dog who was sitting uneasily by his master, a little confused by the hustle and bustle of the shop after six months of clear mountain quiet.

The dog saw the cat flying towards him and, believing himself to be under attack, he readied himself for a fight, keenly observed by the king and minister. When the cat landed just in front of the dog he jumped on her, sinking his teeth into her neck, killing her with one bite of his strong jaws.

'There'll be trouble now!' whispered the minister. 'Shouldn't we do something?' 'No need,' replied the king. 'It's not our problem. Let's just watch and see what happens.' The shopkeeper was furious. The cat was his only mouser. She had kept his shop free from mice and rats for more than ten years. Seeing the cat limp and lifeless in the dog's mouth, he cursed and kicked out at the dog with all his strength, connecting his boot with the dog's head. There was a crunching of bone as the dog's neck snapped.

The minister looked at the king, but he just shrugged back. 'Not our problem,' he mouthed. Now the shepherd loved that dog like an only child, his only companion during the long summer months. When he saw its neck snap he pushed the shopkeeper hard in the chest with his strong arms. The shopkeeper fell backwards, tripped over a box behind him, cracked his skull hard against the stone wall, and fell lifeless to the ground. Fearing for what would happen next the shepherd rushed out of the shop and away towards his flock.

The shopkeeper's son, a patriotic young man, was standing in the doorway of the store as his father slumped to the ground. As the shepherd rushed by, he imagined that his father was dead and called to his friends outside.

'Boys! Catch him! That Westerner just killed my dad!' Inside the store the minster was getting agitated.

'Your majesty, we must do something. The youths are bringing sticks and knives. We should stop this now!'

But the king shook his head.

'Too dangerous,' he said. 'Let's wait till they've calmed down.'

Outside, a crowd of youths pushed the shepherd to the ground, laying into him with their clubs and boots until there was no more life in his bruised and bloody body. When they had finished they turned back towards the shop and saw the shopkeeper standing in the doorway, calling, too late, for them to stop.

News travels fast in the mountains, especially bad news, and it wasn't long before word reached the shepherd's village that he had been killed by a mob of Easterners. Intent on justice, the young men of his village gathered whatever weapons they could muster, crossed over the river and marched up the pass to the nearest Eastern village. When they arrived they found the village empty, its inhabitants fled. The mob eagerly began smashing and burning whatever they could find. Soon the whole village was in flames.

Eastern soldiers were sent to arrest the youths, but when they arrived one of the youths, the cousin of the shepherd, pulled out a pistol and started firing.

The soldiers panicked and, in the confused melee that followed, seventeen Westerners were killed by Eastern bullets.

News got back to the Western rulers that there had been a massacre of their people, and the Western army was sent to the border on full alert with instructions to repel any attacks with full force. The Eastern king sent his own army to the same border with the same instructions, believing the Westerners were preparing for war. For three tense days the armies faced one another across the river, until a young Westerner whose brother had been killed in the melee took a pot shot across the river at some soldiers who had been taunting them. The Eastern platoon fired back and soon both armies were engaged, shooting across the river and fighting hand to hand at the bridges and fords.

In this way a war began which neither king was able to win, yet neither felt able to stop. Each side blamed the other. Each side wanted revenge or compensation. Both peoples rallied around the thought of their victory over evil, convinced that God was on their side. The war raged for ten years until, with both peoples weary of grieving for their lost sons, a truce was finally declared.

When the two kings met to discuss their truce, the Eastern king told the story of what he had seen at the shop.
'If only I had done something about the honey, or the cat or the dog, or the shepherd,' he said, 'then maybe things would have been different.'

The kings declared that the truce day would be named Honey Day and ordered each country to remember this story as a reminder that peace is a precious and fragile thing, that we should all, in our own way, protect.

46. Who is the Husband?

This riddle story is from India.
It opens up discussions about who we are, body and mind and heart.

There were once two brothers, one tall and slim, the other short and tubby. The tall, slim brother was happily married. He loved his wife and she loved him just as much. The other brother was single.

One day the two brothers were walking through a forest when they were attacked by a bandit, who chopped off their heads before stealing their goods.

The tall brother's wife waited and waited, and when her husband didn't turn up she went out into the forest to see what had happened.

She found the two bodies and two heads lying on the ground, and collapsed in shock. She wept and prayed to the goddess Kali, Goddess of Life and Death. 'Mother Kali,' she prayed. 'Please bring my husband back to life. Please!'

The air in front of the wife thickened and swam in front of her eyes as the great goddess appeared in front of her.
'I will grant your request,' she said. 'Replace the heads and I will do the rest.'

And so the wife put back the heads and then waited and watched as the wounds healed and the two men came back to life.

But when the two brothers stood up, the wife noticed something strange. She'd accidentally put the heads onto the wrong bodies. She looked at her husband's head on top of his brother's short, tubby body.

She looked to the brother's head, now on a tall, slim body.

'Oh no!' she thought. 'What have I done? Which one is my husband?' Who do you think is her husband now?

47. What Happens When You Really Listen!

Here's a delightful Indian tale about how stories can change us. Evoke the character of the frustrated wife and maybe the dopey husband, who is somehow energised and transformed by his contact with a story. You can find a version of this and many other similar parables in Pantheon's Folktales from India.

Once there was a wife who found her husband really dull. She decided to do something about it, so she sent him into town to hear a storyteller. The husband sat down in the crowd and began to listen to the stories but was soon fast asleep. While he slept, a dog came by and peed in his mouth. He woke up when the storyteller finished his telling and went home.

'How was that?' asked his wife.

The husband smacked his lips thoughtfully. 'It was a bit salty,' he said. 'Not to my taste.'

His wife thought that didn't sound quite right so she sent him back to see the storyteller again the next night. This time the crowd was even bigger and when the husband fell asleep a man stood on his shoulders to get a better view.
'How was that?' asked his wife when he got home.
'It was a bit heavy for my taste,' he told her.

Again, his wife sent him back. This time the husband stayed awake and listened, enthralled with a story about King Arthur. The storyteller came to the part of the story where King Arthur rode his horse out of the castle and across the drawbridge and dropped his sword, Excalibur, into the moat. The husband was completely absorbed in the story.

He called out, 'Don't worry! I'll help!'

He dived into the moat, swam to the bottom, collected the sword and gave it back to the king then returned to the audience.

When he got home that night his wife asked him, 'How was that?'
'It was great!' he cried. 'I was part of it and I loved it!'

And from that day on, the wife never found her husband dull ever again. That's what happens when you really listen to stories.

48. The Power of Stories

Here's another one from India from the Pantheon collection.
It explores stories and healing and why speaking stories out can be important.

Once there was a woman who lived in a house with her father, her husband and her son.

Every day these three men would tell her to do this, do that, do that, do this, and usually she would do it in sullen silence without ever telling them what she thought.

She kept it all bottled up inside.

One day she went for a walk and came across a ruined cottage without a roof, with just the four walls standing. First, she turned to the north wall and started to shout at it, talking about her father, about all the things he had done, all the things he had said and how she had felt about them but had never said. The power of her words was such that the wall crumbled to the ground.

Then she turned to the east wall and started telling it all about her husband, about all the things he had said, how she felt and so on and so on. The power of her words reduced the wall to rubble.

Then she turned to the south wall and started telling it about her son, about all the things he had said to her in his life and how it had made her feel, and how she had never once said anything. Again the power of her words was so great, the wall collapsed into a pile of bricks.

Finally she turned to the east wall and started to tell it all about herself, about all the things she had never said, all the things she wished for and how she felt about everything. The force of her words collapsed this final wall.

Then she turned around and headed home.
'I feel much better now,' she thought.

49. The Diamond Dream

*This is a challenging fable about letting go of things that cause us pain
– lots to talk about around what is important in life and what makes us happy.
I found this story in David Holt's* More Ready-To-Tell Tales. *It's from India.*

There was once a poor young man who loved diamonds, even though he could never afford one. He loved the way they sparkled, he loved the way they felt, and he loved how much money they were worth.

One night, he dreamed of a forest. In the forest was a hut. In the hut was a hermit and the hermit had a huge and wonderful diamond.

When he woke he recognised the forest and set off to find the hut and perhaps the diamond. He walked and he walked till he came to the forest and then to the hut. He knocked and walked in, and saw a man sitting by the window gazing out at the moon, smiling.

On the floor of that hut was the diamond the man had dreamed about. The diamond was huge and sparkled in the moonlight.

'I'd love to have a diamond like that,' he said.
'Take it, it's yours,' said the man by the window.

The man couldn't believe his luck. He took the diamond home and hid it under the bed. He sat there all night checking that no one was going to steal it. The next day he started to worry about the diamond. Where was he going to put the diamond to keep it safe but where he could also look at it? He bought himself a safe and a gun and kept on worrying about what he was going to do to keep the diamond. His worries grew and grew. He became paler and paler and thinner and thinner.

Finally, weak and ill, he dragged himself back to that forest and that hut, the place he had first found in his dream. He walked in, clutching the diamond to his chest. There at the window was the man who had given him the diamond, still smiling up at the moon.

'I've come back,' said the man.

The man at the window turned to him.

'Why?' he asked.
'There is something I want to learn from you,' said the man, his hands tight around his precious diamond. 'I want you to teach me how to give this diamond away just as you did to me.'

And so he stayed in that hut with that man and studied. In time, the old man died, but the young man remained in the hut with that diamond, gazing happily out at the moon and stars every night.

One day a man walked into his hut and saw the diamond.
'I'd love to have a diamond like that,' he said.

The man at the window turned to the visitor and smiled.
'Take it,' he said.

50. Bird in Hand

I heard this story from storyteller, Eric Maddern.
It's a lovely way of saying, 'Now it's up to you. Take responsibility!'

There was once a son who didn't like his father. He found him proud and pompous and stupid. His father was the village chief and was considered wise and important by the villagers. The son would fume and fume about how annoying his father was and planned to show him up.

At the next village council meeting, he thought, 'I'll catch a bird, hold it between the palms of my hands and walk up to my dad with everyone watching. Then I'll say, "Father, what have I got between my hands?"

'If my dad says, "A bird", then I'll squish the bird between my hands and say, "No, Father. Blood, feathers and bones – see you don't know everything!" and show him the dead bird.

'If my dad says, "Blood, feathers and bones", then I'll open up my hands and show the living bird and say, "Look Father! You are wrong!"'

Either way, the son thought, he would be able to show his father up.

The son waited until there was a very important meeting, found a bird and cupped it between his hands. In front of all of the assembly he said, 'Father, what have I got between my hands?' His father looked at him sadly.

'Son,' he said. 'The answer is in your hands.'

51. Traveller at the Gates of a City

Here's a wonderful little story about transitions and expectations
— a good one for children to take with them to their next school!
Evoke the enigmatic and wise character of the gatekeeper.

A traveller came to the gates of a city. He asked the gatekeeper: 'What are the people like in this place? What's it like to live here?' The gatekeeper replied, 'What was it like in the last place you lived?'

The travelled thought for a moment.
'People were angry and selfish,' he said.
'It will be the same here if you stay,' said the gatekeeper.

Disappointed, the traveller turned around and set off for another town.

A while later a second traveller came to the same gates. He asked the gatekeeper: 'What are the people like in this place? What's it like to live here?' The gatekeeper replied: 'What was it like in the last place you lived?'

The traveller thought for a moment.
'People were happy and kind,' said the traveller.
'It will be the same here if you stay,' said the gatekeeper.

The traveller smiled and walked through the gates, looking for a bed for the night.

Sources and Resources

This section provides more detail on the various sources I drew upon when first learning to tell any given story. Other variants are also included which may be of interest to parents for watching and listening to at home.

There are picture books and storybooks, which may be used to link the story to reading and research activities in various ways, and also web clips and other web resources for children to experience as they go deeper into the story.

The Hunter and the Leopard

This story is known under several names, including *Brave Hunter* and *The Buffalo Woman*. I first heard this told by the wonderful storyteller Jan Blake.

Other Print Versions

Smith, Alexander McCall (1989, 1999, 2004) *The Girl Who Married A Lion and Other Tales From Africa*, Canongate Books, Edinburgh.

Web Sources

Blake, Jan; Sereba, Raymond (2012) The Buffalo Woman hayfestival:

http://www.hayfestival.com/c-209-archive.aspx?ManufacturerFilterID=0&VectorFilterID=4810&GenreFilterID=23

The Boots of Abu Kassim

This comical tale can be found in most of the larger *1001 Nights* translations, although it is often omitted from shorter ones. Also known as *Abu Kassim's Slippers*.

Children's Books

McCaughrean, Geraldine; Fowler, Rosamund (1982) *One Thousand and One Arabian Nights*, Oxford University Press, Oxford.

Other Print Versions

Zimmer, Heinrich; Campbell, Joseph (1948, 1957, 1975) *The King and the Corpse: Tales of the Soul's Conquest of Evil*, Princeton University Press, Princeton, New Jersey.

Who is the Thief?

Children's Books

This story also goes by the name *The Wise Judge* or *A Just Judge*, I first read this in *Ready-to-Tell Tales*, Holt, David; Mooney, Bill; Klein, Susan [1994], August House Inc., Atlanta.

Other Print Versions

Tolstoy, Leo; Blaisdell, Bob; Weiner, Leo; Dole, Nathan (1904, 2001) *Classic Tales and Fables for Children*, Prometheus Books, New York.

Web Sources

Unknown (Accessed online 07/01/2014) *The Young Judge*, Wattpad: http://www.wattpad.com/5143165-wise-short-stories-from-arab-old-times-in-english

Beowulf

There are many retellings of this Anglo-Saxon Classic.

Children's Books

Morpurgo, Michael; Foreman, Michael (2006) *Beowulf,* Walker Books Ltd., London.

Crossley-Holland, Kevin; Keeping, Charles (1999) *Beowulf,* Oxford University Press, Oxford.

Sutcliff, Rosemary; Keeping, Charles (1961, 2001) *Beowulf: Dragonslayer,* Bodley Head, republished by the Random house Group Ltd., London.

Jones, Rob Lloyd; Tavares, Victor (2009) *Beowulf,* Usborne Publishing Ltd., London.

Harris, John; Morgan-Jones, Tom (2007) *The Geat: The Story of Beowulf and Grendel,* notreallybooks, UK.

Nye, Robert (1968, 2004) *Beowulf,* Dolphin, an imprint of Orion Children's Books, a division of the Orion Publishing Group Ltd., London.

Other Print Versions

Heaney, Seamus (2000) *Beowulf: A New Verse Translation,* Farrar, Straus and Giroux, New York.

Alexander, Michael (1973, 2001) *Beowulf: A Verse Translation,* Penguin Group, Penguin Books Ltd, London.

The Tiger's Whisker

This is a much-told tale with many versions in print and on the web. It can be found in both Asia and Africa.

Children's Books

Day, Nancy Raines; Grifalconi, Ann (1995) *The Lion's Whiskers: An Ethiopian Folktale,* Scholastic Trade.

Woods, Rosemary; Mike, Jan M. (2000) *The Lion's Whiskers: An Ethiopian Story*, Pearson Scott Foresman, Pearson Educations Inc., Unkown (US).

Henderson, Kathy Carman (2013) *The Tigers Whisker: A Story to Learn and Draw By*, CreateSpace, Unkown.

Other Print Versions

Courlander, Harold; Arco, Enrico (1995) *The Tiger's Whisker and Other Tales from Asia and the Pacific*, Henry Holt & Company, New York.

Forest, Heather (1996) *Wisdom Tales from Around the World*, August House Inc., Atlanta.

Ashabranner, Brent K.; Davis, Russel G., Siegl, Helen (1997) *The Lion's Whiskers and Other Ethiopian Tales*, Linnet Books, The Shoestring Press Ltd., New Haven.

Web Sources

Ali, Fatima (Accessed online 07/01/2014) *The Woman and the Lion: Ethiopian Folktales*: http:// www.ethiopianfolktales.com/en/benishangul- gumuz/88-the-woman-and-the-lion

The Apple Tree Man

This is a great English standard, occasionally found in collections of Christmas stories for children.

Other Print Versions

Jacksties, Sharon (2012) *Somerset Folktales*, The History Press, Stroud.

Web Sources

Thomas, Taffy (Accessed online 06/01/2014): *The Apple-Tree Man* Wordpress: http://the companyofthegreenman.wordpress.com/2009/01/23/the-apple-tree-man/

Godmother Death

My original source for this tale was Doug Lipman's retelling of a Mexican version in *Ready-to-Tell Tales* (Lipman, Doug; Holt, David; Mooney, Bill [1994] August House Inc., Atlanta). Doug Lipman kindly gave his blessing for the retelling in this book.

Other Print Versions

Wratislaw, Albert Henry (1890) *Sixty Folk-Tales from Exclusively Slavonic Sources,* Houghton, Mifflin and Co., Boston.

Yolen, Jane; Datlow, Ellen; Windling, Terri (1997) *Black Swan, White Raven,* Avon Books, UK.

Web Sources

Traditional (Accessed online 06/01/2014) *The Candles of Life: The Story of a Child for Whom Death Stood Godmother* World Of Tales: http://www.worldoftales.com/ European_folktales/Czechoslovak_folktale_30.html

The Weaver's Dream

Children's Books

Heyer, Marilee (1989) *The Weaving of a Dream,* Puffin Books, imprint of Penguin Books Ltd., London.

San Souci, Robert D.; Gál, Lászlo (1993) *The Enchanted Tapestry,* Puffin Books, London.

Pirotta, Saviour; Johnson, Richard (2007) *Around the World in 80 Tales,* Kingfisher Publications Plc., London.

The Prince and the Birds

I first found this in *Spanish Fairy Tales* (Marks, John; Cook, Hazel [1957] Cladpole Books, West Sussex). There is also a beautiful picture-book version by Amanda Hall (Hall, Amanda [2005] *Prince of the Birds,* Frances Lincoln Ltd, London).

Jumping Mouse

This is a very popular and inspiring Native American story. According to the First People website, its tribal origin is Unknown. I first heard this story years ago from storyteller Katy Cawkwell.

Children's Books

Patten, Brian; Moore, Mary (2010) *Jumping Mouse*, Hawthorn Press, Stroud.

Steptoe, John (1984) *The Story of Jumping Mouse*, William Morrow and Company, Inc., New York.

Web Sources

Forman, Carole (2008) *Jumping Mouse* Youtube: http://www.youtube.com/watch?v=HTZU9hhoT6c

Jack and Jackie

I first heard this from Ben Haggarty, who has told this tale far and wide. I believe it was also told by the great Scottish storyteller Duncan Williamson.

Other Print Versions

Author unknown, many publications in public domain, *22 Goblins*; translated from Sanskrit, 1917, by Ryder, Arthur W.

Web Sources

Martin, Richard (2013) Jimmy No-Story Vimeo: http://vimeo.com/74531121 [Note: video not complete.]

The House That Has Never Known Death

I first found this in Bushnaq's definitive collection *Arab Folktales* (Bushnaq, Inea [1987] Pantheon Books, New York.). There is a similar and well- known legend of the life of Buddha called *The Mustard Seed* or *The Parable of the Mustard Seed*.

Children's Books

Conover, Sarah; Wahl, Valerie (2001, 2011) *Kindness: A Treasury of Buddhist Wisdom for Children and Parents*, Skinner House Books, imprint of the Unitarian Universalist Association, Boston.

Urry, Paul (2004) *Brilliant Stories for Assemblies*, Brilliant Publications, Bedfordshire.

Web Sources

Martin, Richard (2013) *The House That Has Never Known Death* Vimeo: http://vimeo. com/78922641

Ashlimann, D. L. (1999–2002) *The Parable of the Mustard Seed*: http://www.pitt. edu/~dash/mourn. html - mustardseed

Smith, Chris (2013) *The House Which had Never Known Death*, Story Museum: http:// www. storymuseum.org.uk/1001stories/detail/206/the- house-which-had-never-known-death.html

Why the Seagull Cries

This is a Native American Tale attributed to various tribes of the North West Coast. There are a number of more complex versions.

Children's Books

McDermott, Gerald (1993, 2001) Raven: *A Trickster Tale from the Pacific Northwest*, Harcourt, Inc., New York.

Dixon, Ann; Watts, James (1992) *How Raven Brought Light to People*, Margaret K. McElderry Books, imprint of Simon and Schuster Children's Publishing Division, New York.

Web Sources

Traditional (Accessed online 06/01/2014) *How Raven Brought Fire to the Indians*, World of Tales: http://www.worldoftales.com/Native_American_folktales/Native_American_ Folktale_59.html

Traditional (Accessed online 06/01/2014) *Seagull's Daylight Story*, Boy Scout Trail: http:// www.boyscouttrail.com/content/story/seagulls_daylight-1692.asp

Traditional (Accessed online 06/01/2014) *Raven, Seagull and the Coming of Light,* Raven Lore: http://www.shadowraven.org/lore4.htm

Luckily Unlucky

This is a Chinese Taoist tale with many variations. It is sometimes called *A Blessing in Disguise.*

Web Sources

Yang, Jwing-Ming (2007) *A Blessing in Disguise (Chinese Folktale)*, ymaa: http://ymaa. com/articles/ stories-proverbs/blessing-in-disguise

Language Lesson

I can't remember where I first heard this charming story!

Web Sources

Lucy (2010) *Dog as a Second Language* eslpod: http://www.eslpod.com/eslpod_blog/ 2010/01/12/dog-as-a-second-language/

Nasseradeen Tales

These tales and many more can be found in the various collections of stories which go by the names *Nasreddin, Juha* or *Hodja Tales*.

Other Print Versions

Husain, Shahrukh; Archer, Micha (2011) *The Wise Fool: Fables from the Islamic World*, Barefoot Books Ltd., Oxford.

Solovyov, Leonard (1957, 2009) *The Tale of Hodja Nasreddin; Disturber of the Peace*, Translit Publishing, Toronto.

Shah, Idries; Williams, Richard; Cain, Errol Le (1968, 1971, 1993) *The Pleasantries of the Incredible Mulla Nasrudin*, Penguin Books Ltd., Middlesex.

Web Sources

Bashir, Hajji Abdu Settar Mohammed (Accessed online 07/01/2014) *Sheikh Nasreddin in the Rain, Sheikh Nasreddin at the Fork, Sheikh Nasreddin counts the Donkeys, Sheikh Nasreddin and the Miser. Ethiopian Folktales*: http://www.ethiopianfolktales.com/en/harar

Children of Wax

I first heard this from storyteller Michael Moran, who found it in *Children of Wax: African Folk Tales* by Alexander McCall Smith (Smith, Alexander McCall [1989, 1999], Canongate Books, Edinburgh.

Warrior

This popular story often goes by the name *The Black Prince*.

Other Print Versions

Simm, Laura; Holt, David; Mooney, Bill (1994) *Ready-to-Tell Tales*, August House Inc., Atlanta.

Zagloul, Ahmed; Zagloul, Zane; Armstrong, Beverly (1971) *The Black Prince and Other Egyptian Folk Tales*, Doubleday, imprint of Transworld Publishers, Ealing.

Web Sources

Palache, Abbie (2013) Abbie Palache Youtube: http://www.youtube.com/watch?v=ZxvKw5AHJ2E

Baldur

Baldur will be found in most collections of Norse Myths. It's a wonderful story about the beginning of the end.

Children's Books

Ardagh, Philip; May, Steven (1997) *Norse Myths and Legends,* Belitha Press Ltd., imprint of Chrysalis Children's Books, London.

Frith, Alex; Stowell, Louie; Pincelli, Matteo (2013) *Norse Myths*, Usborne Books, Oxon.

Other Print Versions

Crossley-Holland, Kevin (1980, 1982, 1983, 1993, 2011) *Norse Myths: Gods of the Vikings,* Penguin Books Ltd., London.

Picard, Barbara Leonie (1953, 1994, 1996, 2001) *Tales of the Norse Gods*, Oxford University Press, Oxford.

Web Sources

McCoy, Dan (2012, 2014) *The Death of Baldur* Norse Mythology: http://norse-mythology.org/tales/the-death-of-baldur/

Erisython

Also spelt *Erysichthon* and *Erisichthon*, roughly pronounced Err-ees-ick-thon. I particularly enjoy Ted Hughe's version in *Tales from Ovid* (Hughes, Ted [1997] Faber and Faber Ltd, London).

Children's Books

McCaughrean, Geraldine; Clark, Emma Chichester (1999, 20013) *The Orchard Book of Roman Myths*, Orchard Books, London.

Other Print Versions

Fantham, Elaine (2004) *Ovid's Metamorphoses*, Oxford University Press USA, New York.

Quetzalcoatl Brings Chocolate to Earth

Children's Books

Haberstroh, Marilyn and Panik, Sharon (2014) *A Quetzalcoatl Tale of Chocolate*, University Press of Colorado.

Lowery, Linda; Keep, Richard; Porter, Janice Lee (2009) *The Chocolate Tree: A Mayan Folktale*, Millbrook Press, imprint of Lerner Publishins Group, Minneapolis.

Skeleton Woman

This story has become hugely popular with storytellers as a result of its inclusion in the seminal book *Women Who Run With the Wolves: Contacting the Power of the Wild Woman* (Estés, Clarissa Pinkola [1992, 1998, 2008] Rider imprint of Ebury Publishing, a Random House Group Company, London.)

Children's Books

Villoldo, Alberto; Yoshi (2008) *Skeleton Woman*, Simon and Schuster Children's Books, Simon and Schuster, New York.

Web Sources

Pieperhoff, Edith; Morrison, Mary (2004, 2005) *Skeleton Woman*, RedKite Animation: http://redkite-animation.com/_redkite/projects/skeletonwoman/

Smith, Chris (2009-2013) *Skeleton Woman*. Story Museum: www.storymuseum.org. uk/1001-stories/skeleton-woman

The Boy Who Learned to Shudder

Children's Books

Grimm, Wilhelm; Grimm, Jacob (1812) *Children's and Household Tales/Grimm's Fairy Tales*, Not Applicable.

Pullman, Philip (2012) *Grimm Tales for Young and Old*, Penguin Books Ltd., London.

The Woodcutter and the Snake

I first heard this told by Ben Haggarty many years ago.

Other Print Versions

Lee, F.H. (1931) *Folktales From All Nations*, George Harrap and Co. Ltd, London.

Mother Sun and Her Daughters

I found this story in a wonderful collection called *Primal Myths: Creation Myths Around the World* (Sproul, Barbara C. [1992] HarperOne, imprint of Harper Collins Publishers, San Francisco).

Five Wise Trainings

I came across this tale in one of Andrew Lang's collections. He calls it *The Five Wise Words of the Guru*.

Other Print Versions

Lang, Andrew (1907) *The Olive Fairy Book*, Longmans, Green and Co, London. Now in the Public Domain.

Web Sources

Lang, Andrew (Accessed online 08/01/2014) *The Five Wise Words of the Guru*, Sacred-Texts: http://www.sacred-texts.com/neu/lfb/ol/olfb16.htm

Gawain Gets Married

This is another classic of Arthurian legend with many literary retellings.

Children's Books

Courtauld, Sarah; Davidson, Susanna; Daynes, Katie; Dickins, Rosie; Punter, Russel; Sebag-Montefore, Mary; Sims, Lesley (several editions) *One Hundred Illustrated Stories*, Usborne Children's Books, Usborne, Books Ltd., London.

Hastings, Selina; Wijngaard, Juan (1985,1987) *Sir Gawain and the Loathly Lady*, Walker Books Ltd., London.

Ashley, Mike (2005) *The Mammoth Book of King Arthur*, Constable and Robinson Ltd., London.

Other Print Versions

Hahn, Thomas (1995) *Sir Gawain: Eleven Romances and Tales*. Medieval Institute Publications, Kalamazoo, Michigan.

Everything You Need

This rather harsh salutary tale was collected by C.G. Campbell in Iraq in the 1930s.

Children's Books

Campbell, C. G.; Buckland-Wright, John (1949, 1980, 2008) *Tales from the Arab Tribes*, Lindsay Drummond Ltd., Unknown, Arno Press, New York.

Gilgamesh

I first heard this told by Ben Haggarty, whose storytelling of this tale was truly inspirational. There are many translations and versions of what is possibly the oldest surviving written story.

Children's Books

McCaughrean, Geraldine; Parkins, David (2002) *Gilgamesh the Hero: The Oldest Story Ever Told*, Oxford University Press, Oxford.

Other Print Versions

Mitchell, Stephen (2004) *Gilgamesh: A New English Version,* Profile Books Ltd., London.

Bryson, Bernarda (1966, 2012) *Gilgamesh: Man's First Story,* Pied Piper Press, Sacramento.

George, Andrew (1999) *The Epic of Gilgamesh,* Penguin Books Ltd., London.

A Drop of Honey

This story is in many 1001 Arabian Nights collections, and variations of it can be found in Burma, Thailand and Iran.

Other Print Versions

Macdonald, Margaret Read (1992) *Peace Tales,* August House Inc., Atlanta.

Aung, Maung Htin; Trager, Helen G.; Tiset, Paw Oo (1968) *A Kingdom Lost for a Drop of Honey And Other Burmese Folktales,* Parent's Magazine Press, Unknown.

Web Sources

Heathfield, David (Accessed online 23/01/2014) *The Drop of Honey,* World Stories: http://www.worldstories.org.uk/stories/story/35-the-drop-of-honey

Chand, Peter (209-2014) *A Drop of Honey,* Story Museum: www.storymuseum.org.uk/1001-stories/a-drop-of-honey

Who is the Husband?

This story comes from an ancient Indian collection of riddle tales. I found it in *22 Goblins,* author unknown, many publications in public domain; translated from Sanskrit, 1917, by Ryder, Arthur W.

What Happens When You Really Listen!

I found this delightful tale in Folktales from India: *A Selection of Oral Tales from Twenty-Two Languages* (Ramanujan, A. K. [1991] Pantheon Books, a division of Random House Inc., New York. Simultaneously published by Random House of Canada Ltd., Toronto.)

Other Print Versions

Richman, Paula (1991) *Many Ramayanas: The Diversity of a Narrative Tradition in South Asia*, University of California Press, Berkeley and Los Angeles.

Web Sources

Richman, Paula (1991) Many Ramayanas: *The Diversity of a Narrative Tradition in South Asia*: cdlib: http://publishing.cdlib.org/ucpressebooks/view?docId=ft3j49n8h7&chunk. id=d0e3172&toc. depth=100&brand=eschol

Smith, Chris (2009-2014) *What Happens When You Really Listen*, Story Museum: https://www.storymuseum.org.uk/1001-stories/what-happens-when-you-really-listen

The Diamond Dream

I first came across this in a version by Jim May called *The Ruby* (May, Jim; Holt, David; Mooney, Bill [2000] *More Ready-to-Tell Tales From Around the World*, August House Inc., Atlanta.). Jim kindly approved my retelling in this book.

Bird in Hand

I first heard this story from storyteller Eric Maddern. It was also used by Toni Morrison in her acceptance speech when receiving the Nobel Prize in Literature. Trauma specialist Mooli Lahad uses a version with a butterfly and therapist in his book below.

Other Print Versions

Lahad, Mooli (2000) *Creative Supervision: The Use of Expressive Arts Methods in Supervision and Self-Supervision*, Jessica Kingsley Publishing, London and Philadelphia.

Jaffe, Nina; Zeitlin, Steve; Segal, John (1993) *While Standing on One Foot: Puzzle Stories and Wisdom Tales from the Jewish Tradition*, Henry Holt and Company LLC, New York.

Kornfield, Jack; Feldman, Christina (1991) *Soul Food: Stories to Nourish the Spirit and the Heart*, HarperOne, imprint of Harper Collins Publishers, San Francisco.

Bartholome, Paula; Wacker, Mary B.; Silverman, Lori L. (2003) *Stories Trainers Tell: 55 Ready-to-Use Stories to Make Training Stick*, Pfeiffer, imprint of John Wiley and Sons Inc., San Francisco.

Traveller at the Gates of a City

I came across this great little tale in *Soul Food: Stories to Nourish the Spirit and Heart* (Kornfield, Jack; Feldman, Christina [1996] HarperCollins, San Francisco.)

Web Sources

Ashliman, D.L. (Accessed online 23/01/2014) *The Traveler and the Farmer*, Pitt.Edu: http://www.pitt.edu/~dash/traveltales.html

Acknowledgements

The stories in this collection are all traditional stories that have evolved over the centuries by being told and retold over and over again. Behind all these tales stand tens of thousands of storytellers who have adapted the tales to suit their own styles and purposes, all part of the still-evolving story.

Many of these stories are quite popular in England, told by storytellers in schools, festivals and story circles throughout the country. I have told all of these stories myself and tried to bring my own storyteller's voice to the written text. However, doubtless I have picked up phrases and ideas from others, as is the way with traditional stories, so thanks to all the tellers of these tales whom I have seen and heard over the years.

I'd like to name a few storytellers who have been particularly inspiring and influential to me over the years, and whose voices I have no doubt sought to imitate and integrate into my own telling. Thanks to Ben Haggarty, Daniel Morden, Hugh Lupton, Jan Blake, Sally Pomme Clayton, Vergine Gulbenkian and Eric Maddern. Thanks to Lucy and Claire at Hawthorn Press for making the book happen, and in particular to Martin Large for his support and advice. Thanks to the Story Museum, Oxford for generously helping with the editing of earlier drafts of this collection. Much appreciation to Alida Gersie and Hugh Lupton for their advice and feedback when preparing this book.

Finally, I'd like to acknowledge the stories themselves. They come alive when told and retold out loud. They like to be shared, changed, played around with and enjoyed. With your help, may they go forth and multiply.

About the Author

Chris Smith PhD

Chris Smith PhD, is a storyteller, educational trainer and founding Director of Storytelling Schools. Chris loves helping to make education more joyful, effective and engaging, especially in areas of social deprivation where good education can make such a difference to future life chances. For the last twenty years Chris has been researching and developing the Storytelling Schools idea in UK schools. Chris has also been a father, musician, exhibition designer, performer, monk, UN manager, human ecologist, surfer and writer. He currently divides his time between a home in Gloucestershire and a wood in Devon.

Storytelling Schools™ is an educational method where oral storytelling is placed at the heart of learning. Our model integrates elements from the creative arts and educational sciences into a whole school method in a lively, dynamic and inclusive way. Educators using our method report huge gains in both academic and personal development. In this approach, oracy and creativity provide the springboards for learning both language and subject content across the curriculum. We provide resources, support and training to organisations and individuals wishing to adopt the method.

For more information visit www.storytellingschools.com

storytelling schools
where every child is a storyteller

Other Titles from Storytelling Schools

The Storytelling Schools Method: Handbook for Teachers

Chris Smith, Adam Guillain & Kate Barron
Foreword by Pie Corbett

The handbook is aimed at early years, primary school and middle school teachers as well as home educators. Students learn to be storytellers, performing pieces as a way of internalising language, structure and meaning in a simple and engaging way.

ISBN: 9798665184807 Paperback, Twinberrow Publishing

147 Storytelling Games and Creative Activities for the Classroom and the Home

Chris Smith PhD & Kate Barron MEd

This collection provides a clear, concise and rich source of ideas for how to learn and play through storytelling. Sections include speaking and listening games, learning to tell a story, drama, movement, music, poetry, writing, story recycling and story creation. The book is suitable for classroom teachers, early years workers, home educators, team leaders and anyone who wants to play around with stories in a creative and engaging way.

ISBN: 9798634803173 Paperback, Twinberrow Publishing

Stories for this Uncertain Time
Tales and Creative Activities for Teachers and Parents to Help Children Adapt

Chris Smith PhD

All around the world children are learning to adapt to the new realities of the COVID-19 pandemic. This story collection will help primary aged children to better understand the science of the pandemic, their own personal responses and the key behaviours that can keep them and their communities safer.

ISBN: 9798649515276 Paperback, Twinberrow Publishing

All books available via: www.storytellingschools.com/bookshop

World Tales
for Family Storytelling
by Chris Smith
from Hawthorn Press

'Carefully collected by Chris Smith, and honed down to perfect gems of storytelling – simple, and memorable, they encourage all of us to become family storytellers.'
Jamila Gavin

These wonderful world tales are all selected from the highly acclaimed *147 Traditional Stories for Primary School Children to Retell*, a reference book used by teachers around the globe. Retelling a story from memory will help your children master new language, ideas and emotions and encourage creativity while building their confidence in communication. In these three books for home use, the stories are to share within your family in whatever way you choose: read them, tell them from memory, change them, re-enact them, discuss them, paint them, play with them and above all get your family to engage with them.

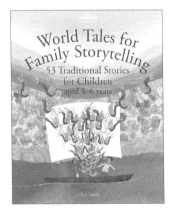

World Tales for Family Storytelling I
53 Stories for Children aged 4–6 years
ISBN: 978-1-912480-55-5

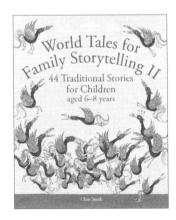

World Tales for Family Storytelling II
44 Stories for Children aged 6–8 years
ISBN: 978-1-912480-66-1

Making the Children's Year

Seasonal Waldorf Crafts with Children

Marije Rowling

Drawing on the creative ethos of Steiner Waldorf education, this is a full-colour second edition of *The Children's Year.* Packed with all kinds of seasonal crafts, for beginners and experienced crafters, this book is a gift for parents seeking to make toys that will inspire children and provide an alternative to throwaway culture.

240pp; 250 x 200mm; paperback; ISBN 978-1-907359-69-9

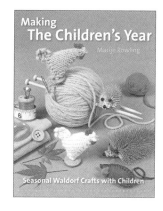

The Children's Forest

Dawn Casey, Anna Richardson, Helen d'Ascoli

A rich and abundant treasury in celebration of the outdoors, this book encourages children's natural fascination with the forest and its inhabitants. An enchanting book where imagination, story and play bring alive the world of the forest. Full of games, facts, celebrations, craft activities, recipes, foraging, stories and Forest School skills. Ideal for ages 5–12, it will be enjoyed by all ages.

336pp; 200 × 250mm; paperback with flaps; ISBN 978-1-907359-91-0

The Natural Storyteller

Wildlife Tales for Telling

Georgiana Keable

Here is a handbook for the natural storyteller, with story maps, brain-teasing riddles, story skeletons and adventures to make a tale your own. Georgiana Keable shows through a range of techniques – sometimes the power of the story alone – how to interpret, re-tell and pass these stories on for the future. This diverse collection of stories will nurture active literacy skills and help form an essential bond with nature.

272pp; 228 x 186mm; paperback; ISBN 978-1-907359-80-4

Making Needle Felted Animals

Over 20 wild, domestic and imaginary creatures
Steffi Stern, Sophie Buckley

The projects in this essential guide arise from a genuine love of the natural world and animals. The instructions are easy to follow and include practical yet creative ideas to fix common mistakes. Requiring no experience other than an interest in working and playing with wool, projects progressively build on skills throughout and will transform you into an avid needle-felter.

128pp; 250 x 200mm; paperback; ISBN 978-1-907359-46-0

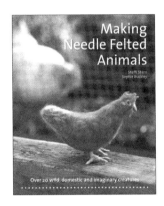

Games Children Play II

Games to develop social skills, teamwork, balance and coordination
Kim John Payne and Cory Waletzko

A companion to the *Waldorf Games Handbook for the Early Years*, *Games Children Play II* uses the Waldorf Spatial Dynamics approach with 237 games to develop children's spatial awareness, social skills, confidence and movement in age-appropriate ways. Each game is clearly and simply described, with diagrams and drawings for how to play.

264pp; 246 x 189mm; paperback; ISBN 978-1-912480-52-4

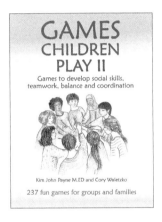

Ordering Books

If you have difficulties ordering Hawthorn Press books from a bookshop,
you can order direct from our website www.hawthornpress.com,
or from our UK distributor BookSource: 50 Cambuslang Road, Glasgow, G32 8NB,
Tel: (0845) 370 0063, E-mail: orders@booksource.net.

Details of our overseas distributors can be found on our website.

Hawthorn Press

www.hawthornpress.com